Joyce Dawe

Patchworkduett

Patchwork mit pfiffigen Applikationen

Joyce Dawe

Patchworkduet

Patchwork enriched with Appliqué

Bergtor Verlag

Herausgeber und Lektorat: BERGTOR VERLAG GmbH, Grünstadt
Übersetzung: Astrid Reck
Fotos: Markus Witt
Grafiken: Barbara Klotz
Umschlagentwurf: Astrid Reck
Layout, Satz und Repro: Satz & Service, Hildegard Pauluweit, Filderstadt
Druck: AALEXX Druck GmbH, Großburgwedel

ISBN 3-937703-09-8

Publisher: BERGTOR VERLAG GmbH, Grünstadt
Translated by: Astrid Reck
Photography: Markus Witt
Graphics: Barbara Klotz
Cover design: Astrid Reck
Layout, Typography and Reproduction: Satz & Service, Hildegard Pauluweit, Filderstadt
Printed by: AALEXX Druck GmbH, Großburgwedel

ISBN 3-937703-09-8

Ich widme dieses Buch meinen geliebten Enkeln Thomas Kent, Bryn Williams und Owen Williams, das neueste Mitglied des Teams, der gerade rechtzeitig kam, um seinen Namen hier veröffentlicht zu bekommen.

I wish to dedicate this book to my much-loved grandchildren, Thomas Kent and Bryn Williams (my boys) and to the newest member of the team, Owen Williams, who arrived just in time to have his name printed here.

Danksagung

Vielen Dank meinem Ehemann Lawrence für die Reinschrift meiner Kritzeleien und das Reinzeichnen meiner Skizzen mit Hilfe des Computerprogramms Quilt Pro und auch für seine allgemeine Unterstützung.

Joanna und Judith danke ich dafür, dass sie Töchter sind, auf die ich stolz sein kann und dafür, dass sie in meine Patchwork Fußstapfen getreten sind, um nicht zu sagen, dass sie mich auf diesem Weg überholen.

Und ganz wichtig ist natürlich mein Dank an den BERGTOR VERLAG, besonders an Astrid und Gaby, dafür, dass sie genug Vertrauen in meine Fähigkeiten hatten, um dieses Buch auf den Weg zu bringen. Ohne sie wäre es nie zustande gekommen.

Acknowledgment

I would like to thank my husband, Lawrence, for transcribing and sorting out my scribblings and redrawing my diagrams with the aid of Quilt-Pro Computer Design programme and for his general support.

Joanna and Judith for being daughters to be proud of and following very much in my patchwork footsteps (if not overtaking me!).

And of course, very importantly to BERGTOR VERLAG, especially Astrid and Gaby for having enough faith in my abilities to commission this book. It would not have happened without them.

Inhaltsverzeichnis

Table of Contents

Einführung

Mit diesem Buch möchte ich zeigen, dass jede Designidee auf mehrere Arten ausgeführt werden kann. Meist kann man eine Idee ausbauen und viel mehr daraus machen als nur einen Quilt. Oftmals nähen wir ein Quiltobjekt und werfen die Schablonen weg, wenn wir mit dem nächsten Projekt anfangen. Wir alle haben mehrere Uvos (unvollendete Objekte) and mindestens noch einmal doppelt so viele Ideen im Kopf – unsere Kreativität übersteigt unsere tatsächliche Produktion. Sie benötigen ein gutes Ordnungssystem, um alle Details von all Ihren Projekten zu dokumentieren, denn jede Idee kann ausgebaut und noch einmal neu und anders in der Zukunft genutzt werden. Momentan arbeite ich an einem Quilt, dessen Muster ich schon vor 10 Jahren benutzt habe. Ich ging mit einem ganz neuen Ansatz daran und fand es sehr praktisch, dass die Schablonen schon fix und fertig auf mich gewartet haben.

In diesem Buch finden Sie insgesamt 12 Projekte, jedes mit Bildern und Vorschlägen für eine Alternative. Für jedes der 12 Projekte gibt es eine Anleitung. Der Titelquilt ist zusätzlich beschrieben. Ich hoffe, dass die Entwürfe Sie zu noch mehr eigenen Ideen inspirieren.

Introduction

My basic idea for this book is to show how to use one design in at least two ways, in other words to expand on one single idea. So often we make one quilted item and discard all the templates before embarking on the next project. We all have several UFO's (Unfinished Objects) and at least double that number in our head – our enthusiasms overtake our makings! You need a good filing system – just to keep every detail of anything you make – because every idea can be expanded and used in a different form for the future. I am currently working on a quilt from some patterns I used 10 years ago using a different approach to the idea and it has been so useful to find the templates already made and waiting for me.

There are 12 projects in all with instructions for one item of each project, accompanied by pictures and suggestions for an alternative idea for each. For the coverquilt you will find an additional description. I hope the designs will inspire you to lead to yet more ideas of your own.

Joyce Dawe

Allgemeine Anleitungen

In diesem Kapitel beschreibe ich meine bevorzugten Arbeitsmethoden. Es gibt so viele verschiedene Techniken des Zusammennähens, der Applikation, des Einfassens von Quilts und der Fertigstellung von Kissen, etc. und keine davon ist die Beste. Die beste Methode ist immer die, die Ihnen selbst am besten liegt. Wenn Sie also eine andere Technik als meine nutzen wollen, kein Problem, tun Sie es einfach! Dies sollen nur einige hilfreiche Tipps sein, mit denen ich meine Arbeitsweise illustrieren möchte.

Patchwork nähen (piecing)

Ich mache für jedes benötigte Teil Schablonen. Die Schablonen werden auf die linke Stoffseite gelegt und mit einem Bleistift umfahre ich die Konturen der Schablone. Dies ist dann die Nählinie – die wichtigste Linie. Ich schneide mit einem Minimum von 0,6 cm (1/4") Nahtzugabe aus, niemals weniger – größere Nahtzugaben können jederzeit zurück geschnitten werden. Zwei Stoffstücke jeweils rechts auf rechts legen und stecken. Auf der Nählinie nähen. Dabei nicht einfach nach Gefühl vorgehen, sondern immer schön kontrollieren, ob die Nählinien auch genau aufeinander liegen. Die Ausnahme in diesem Buch ist der Tischläufer *Spiel mit Blocks,* wofür ich das Nahtzugabenmaß an der Nähmaschine genutzt habe. Aber es ist schon erstaunlich, wie ungenau man nähen kann, auch wenn es eigentlich nicht passieren sollte. Es gibt ja auch extra eine Kontrollschablone, mit der man überprüfen kann, ob die zweifarbigen Quadrate auch akkurat sind. Wenn man von Hand näht, sollte man nicht über die Nählinie hinaus nähen. Wenn man mit der Maschine näht, kann man von Kante zu Kante nähen. Zuerst kleine Einheiten nähen, die man dann mit weiteren kleinen Einheiten zu größeren Einheiten zusammenfügt.

Applizieren

Es gibt so viele Methoden, aus denen man wählen kann. Ich appliziere meist von Hand. Ich stelle eine Schablone her für die zu applizierenden Teile, lege sie auf die rechte Stoffseite und mar-

General Instructions

This chapter is purely notes on my favoured methods of working. There are so many different ways to piece patchwork, appliqué shapes, bind quilts, finish cushions etc. and no particular approach alone is the best – the best is what suits each individual, so, if you prefer to use any method you have already been taught please go ahead. These are mainly some helpful hints illustrating the way I like to work.

Patchwork Piecing

I make templates for each component part. Place templates on the reverse side of my chosen fabrics and mark all round with a pencil. This represents the sewing line – the most important line. I then cut out shapes with a minimum of 1/4" seam allowance. It can be a little more but never less – large seam allowances can always be trimmed down neatly. Pin together right sides of 2 pieces to be joined and sew on the sewing line. I do not guess that the bottom line matches the top and I look from front to back to check that the two pieces are aligned correctly. The exception in this book is the *Block Play Table Runner* where I have used the 1/4" line measurement on the sewing machine, but it is amazing how inaccurate one can be, even though it should not happen, and there is a checking template to make sure the half-square triangular squares are correct. When piecing by hand, the sewing should be exactly the sewing line and not extending into seam allowances either side. When piecing by machine the sewing can be completely from edge to edge. Build up small areas first, which can then be joined to other small areas to make the whole.

Appliqué

There are just so many methods to choose from. I mostly hand appliqué. I make a template shape of the piece to be applied, place on RIGHT side of chosen fabric and draw round with a pencil.

kiere die Konturen mit einem Bleistift. Ich schneide mit einer knappen Nahtzugabe von eher 1/8" (0,3 cm) als einem 1/4" (0,6 cm) aus. Es sei denn, es handelt sich um ein Stück, das später ganz klar von einem anderen Teil überlappt wird. Da ist es hilfreich, wenn man die Nahtzugabe etwas größer wählt. Beim Applizieren kann man leichter mogeln als beim normalen Zusammennähen, denn es fällt nicht weiter auf, wenn man die Position nicht ganz genau einhält.

Bevor ich ans Festnähen gehe, falte ich jedes Stück entlang der Bleistiftlinie, außer natürlich bei Stücken, die überlappt werden. Bei den Stellen, die überlappt werden, schneide ich die Nahtzugaben für die angrenzenden umgefalteten Stellen ein bisschen ein, damit es keinen unschönen Wulst gibt und die Nahtzugaben schön flach liegen können. Kurven sollten innerhalb der Nahtzugaben bis kurz vor die Bleistiftlinie eingeschnitten werden. Ich platziere immer erst alle Teile auf dem Hintergrund, um das fertige Bild zu sehen, dann nehme ich alle Stücke bis auf die ersten wieder weg und stecke diese fest. Zum Applizieren falte ich die Nahtzugabe soweit unter die Bleistiftlinie, dass diese ebenfalls verschwindet und nähe sie mit einem unsichtbaren Applikationsstich fest. Das Garn sollte immer die gleiche Farbe haben wie das aufgenähte Teil, nicht wie der Hintergrund. Nach und nach die weiteren Teile auflegen, fest stecken und annähen. Dies ist ein etwas lockerer Ansatz als alle Umrisse auf den Hintergrund zu zeichnen, aber bei mir klappt das gut so.

Zum Applizieren mit der Nähmaschine werden die selben Schablonen benutzt, allerdings ohne Nahtzugabe. Die Stücke kann man mit verschiedenen Zierstichen oder einem engen Zick-Zack-Stich fest nähen. Hilfreich ist dabei die Verwendung eines Klebevlieses wie Vliesofix oder Steam-a-Seam. Genaue Gebrauchsanweisungen liegen dem Produkt meist bei.

Selbstgemachte Schrägstreifen

Zum Herstellen von Schrägstreifen, zum Beispiel für keltische Designs, benutze ich weder ein Hilfsmittel noch bügele ich die Streifen. Ich schneide die Streifen dreimal so breit wie die fertige Breite. Wenn ich einen Streifen von 0,6 cm

Cut out with a small seam allowance, closer to 1/8" than a 1/4", except where it is obvious that one appliqué piece will overlap another and then it is more helpful to have the 1/4" seam allowance. Appliqué is very forgiving and, unlike piecing patchwork, it is possible to be slightly out of position! Before sewing I take each fabric piece and fold over on the drawn line, with the exception of any overlapped areas, where a scissor snip in the seam allowance will allow for the underneath section to remain flat. Curves should be snipped with scissors within the seam allowance to just short of the folded edge. I position all pieces in place on the background fabric to represent the finished result, remove all but the first basic shapes and tack in place. Turn under on the lightly folded pencil line and slip stitch, using a thread colour to match each individual appliqué piece, not the background colour. Add subsequent shapes to build up the whole appliquéd area. This is a more casual approach than drawing the outlines onto the background piece or using an overlay, but I find it works for me.

Machine appliqué uses the same templates but the applied shape is cut exactly on the drawn line and can be machine zig-zagged, top stitched or hem stitched with the help of an adhesive webbing like Bondaweb. Clear instructions on how to use these adhesive webbings come with the products.

Self Made Bias Strips

The method I use for making bias tapes, for example for Celtic work, does not use any gizmo or ironing. I cut bias strips 3 times the width I want the width to finish with and make two folds to the inside along the length. If I want a

(1/4") Breite möchte, schneide ich den Streifen 1,8 cm (3/4") breit. Die Kanten falte ich der Länge nach links auf links zur Mitte und reihe sie ein. Dann appliziere ich sie entlang beider Kanten auf den Hintergrund. Die Reihstiche entferne ich, wenn der Streifen festgenäht ist.

Wenn lange Streifen benötigt werden, füge ich sie wie in der Zeichnung mit einer Nahtzugabe von 0,6 cm (1/4") zusammen.

Für ein keltisches Muster werden normalerweise nur kurze Stücke benötigt, da man die Anfangs- und Endstücke unter einem kreuzenden Streifen verstecken kann.

strip 1/4" wide, I cut a bias strip 3/4" wide. I then tack these folds in place and slip stitch either side to the background piece. No ironing before appliquéing is necessary and tacking is removed when strip is stitched in place.

When long strips are required I join before folding with a 1/4" seam.

When appliquéing a Celtic design, it would only be necessary to have shorter lengths of bias, as starting and finishing can be hidden under a crossing point.

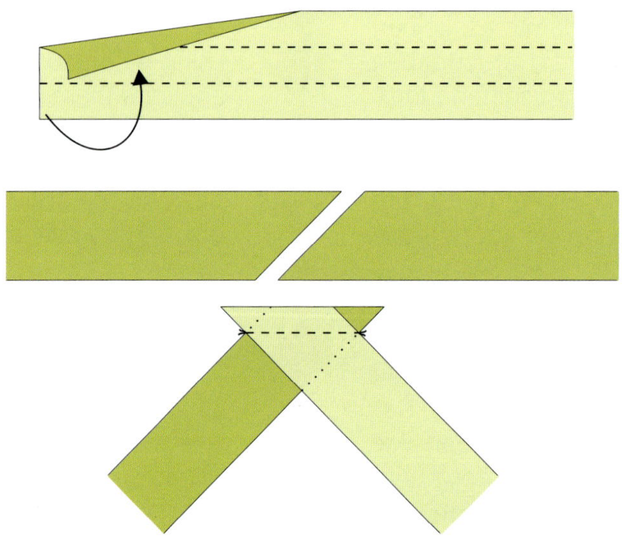

Reversapplikation

Diese Art der Applikation erfordert ein geradliniges Design und zwei Stoffe. Die beiden Stoffe links auf rechts legen, so dass beide mit der rechten Seite oben liegen. Der Hauptstoff mit der aufgezeichneten Linie sollte auf dem anderen Stoff liegen. Die aufgezeichnete Linie ein kleines Stück weit aufschneiden, die Kanten nach unten falten und festnähen. Zuerst nur auf einer Seite arbeiten und nicht gleich alles aufschneiden. Immer nur stückchenweise schneiden. Dann die zweite Seite bearbeiten.

Reverse Appliqué

This requires a linear design and two fabrics. Place one fabric on top of the second, both facing upwards, the main fabric on top with the drawn linear design. Cut on the drawn line a little way, turn under edges and slip stitch in place. Work one side first and do not cut the entire line, just cut as you go, then complete second side.

Markieren

In den allermeisten Fällen benutze ich einen Bleistift. Nur auf sehr dunklen Stoffen verwende ich einen weißen Stift. Empfehlenswert ist ein Bleistift der Stärke H und nicht ein weicher Bleistift B, denn der neigt zum Verschmieren. Bei keltischen Designs zeichne ich nur eine Linie auf und platziere die Schrägstreifen genau auf dieser Linie, so dass sie komplett verdeckt wird. Wie schon vorher erwähnt, markiere ich bei Patchwork Schablonen immer auf der linken Stoffseite, aber bei Applikationsschablonen immer auf der rechten Stoffseite. Auch Quiltlinien zeichne ich mit Bleistift auf, aber nur sehr leicht, gerade so, dass ich die Linie erkennen kann. Manchmal zeichne ich auch nur gestrichelte Linien – aber niemals richtig dicke Linien.

In diesem Buch geht es hauptsächlich um Designs und nicht so sehr um die verschiedenen Methoden. Ich hoffe trotzdem, dass Ihnen diese Erläuterungen weiter helfen.

Marking

I use a lead pencil on most fabrics, but a white pencil on very dark fabrics. Use an H pencil not a soft B because of smudging. When making Celtic designs I draw only one line and place bias fabric strips centrally on this line. As mentioned earlier I draw round all patchwork templates on the wrong side of fabrics and all round appliqué templates on the right side of the fabric. I mark quilting designs also in pencil but very, very lightly just enough for me to be able to see and sometimes dashed lines never scored heavy marking.

This is essentially a book of designs rather than an encyclopaedia of methods, I do hope all the above will prove useful.

Versteckte Katzen / *Hidden Cats*

42 x 48 cm (16 1/2" x 19 1/2")

Jeder von uns hat schon einmal eine Katze beobachtet, die sich im Gebüsch oder Gras versteckt und auf eine Bewegung ihrer Beute wartet. Aber natürlich ist die Katze nicht wirklich unsichtbar. Oftmals sind es ihre leuchtenden Augen, die sie verraten. Um die Katze auf dem Hintergrund zu verstecken, benutzen wir die Reversapplikation. Die Durchbrüche im Katzenkörper lassen die Katze scheinbar mit ihrer Umgebung verschmelzen.

We have all seen cats hiding in the undergrowth watching out for any slight movement from their intended prey. But of course they are not really invisible and often it's their bright eyes that give them away. Cut parts of this outline away using reverse appliqué, and try to hide them.

Stoffbedarf

Katze und Borte: 30 x 110 cm (12" x 44")
Hintergrund: 4 verschiedene Batikstreifen von jeweils 35,6 cm (14") Länge und 10,2 cm (4"), 9 cm (3 1/2), 7 cm (3 1/4"), 4,5 cm (1 3/4") Breite
Augen: Batikreste und Silber- oder Metallicreste
Außerdem: Freezer Paper für die Katzenschablone

Schablonen (s. Seite 15)

Schablone A und B für die Applikation herstellen, Schablone C zum Quilten.

Schneiden und nähen

Vom Stoff für die Katze ein Stück von 23 x 28 cm (9" x 11") schneiden, den Rest in Streifen von 7,5 cm (3") Breite für die Borte schneiden.
Jeweils 8 Stücke A (Batik) und B (Metallic) für die Augen ausschneiden.

Die Umrisse der Katze auf das Freezer Paper übertragen. Ausschneiden, auch alle mit X markierten Stücke ausschneiden. Jeweils auf der Linie schneiden. Die Katzenschablone mit der glänzenden Freezer Paper Seite auf den Stoff bügeln. Mit einem hellen Stift alle Umrisse nachfahren. Freezer Paper entfernen und die Katze ausschneiden, dabei nach Augenmaß ca. 0,5 cm (3/16") Nahtzugabe zugeben. Noch nicht die Stücke innerhalb der Katze ausschneiden!

Die vier Batikstreifen der Länge nach in beliebiger Reihenfolge zusammennähen. Der schmalste Streifen sollte jedoch nicht außen liegen.

Katzenform in der Mitte dieses Hintergrunds platzieren und einreihen. Die Nahtzugabe nach unten falten und mit farblich zur Katze passendem Garn rund herum applizieren. Jetzt die innen liegenden Teile nach und nach ausschneiden, Nahtzugabe nicht vergessen, und fest nähen. Kleine senkrechte Stiche auf die Metallicaugenteile sticken. Metallicteile auf die Batikaugen applizieren. Komplette Augen beliebig auf dem Hintergrund platzieren und festnähen. Bortenstreifen zuerst links und rechts annähen, dann oben und unten. Wie üblich einreihen und quilten.

Fabric requirements

Cat and Borders: 12" x 44"
Background: 4 strips of Batik fabric, 4", 3 1/2", 3 1/4", 1 3/4" wide and 14" long each
Eyes: Batik scraps, silver or metallic scraps for inner eyes.
Freezer Paper for cat outline.

Construction

From the cat and border fabric cut 1 piece 9" x 11" for cat body and cut remainder into 3" wide strips for border.
Transfer cat design onto freezer paper sheet.
Cut round outside of cat shape on the freezer paper and cut out all pieces marked 'X' within the shape – cutting on the drawn lines in all cases.

Iron the cat shape, shiny side down onto RIGHT side of 9" x 11" piece. Mark with white or light pencil round all lines. Remove freezer paper and cut round OUTSIDE of body shape, adding 3/16" all round for seam allowance.

DO NOT cut out inside "tabby" shapes on fabric at this point.

Sew the 4 Batik strips lengthwise in any order you choose but make sure the narrowest strip is not an edge piece. For guidance the strips in the illustrated wallhanging are placed in the following order: 3 1/4", 4", 1 3/4" and 3 1/2"
But do experiment to see which arrangements you prefer.

Centralize the cat fabric shape onto the pieced Batik strips and tack to hold in position. Turn under the seam allowance and appliqué all around the outside of the cat shape, using thread to match the cat fabric. Cut away each inside 'tabby' area one at a time, ADDING 3/16" seam each time. Turn under seam allowance and appliqué round each shape as before, exposing the fabrics beneath.

Sew on 3" border strips previously reserved, firstly on each side, then top and bottom.

Quilten

Die Umrisse aller applizierten Teile betonen, auch die ausgesparten Innenteile des Katzenkörpers. Für die Borte wurde die Augenschablone C verwendet. Dazu auf allen Bortenseiten die Mitte markieren und von dort ausgehend die Schablone so auflegen, dass immer die spitzen Enden aneinander stoßen. In der Mitte der jeweiligen Seiten überlappen die Linien. Nach dem Quilten wie üblich schließen und einen Tunnel annähen.

Templates (page 15)

Make templates A and B for eyes and C for quilting pattern. Using eye template A and scraps of Batik fabrics, cut 8 shapes PLUS 3/16" seam allowance. Using eye template B and metallic or shiny fabrics cut 8 shapes plus 3/16" seam allowance. Appliqué these smaller eye shapes onto the larger Batik eye shapes. Embroider a single vertical line in the centre of each to resemble a cat's eye, then appliqué each entire eye shape in various positions onto background.

Quilting

Tack top, wadding and backing together. Quilt round outside of cat, within each 'tabby' inside shape and around all eye appliqués. Mark centre of each border and starting at each corner, using template C, mark quilting design along border, placing template end to end to make a continuous sewing line. Overlap design as necessary at marked centre. Quilt marked border.
Complete the wallhanging with the binding and adding a 3" sleeve on the back at the top.

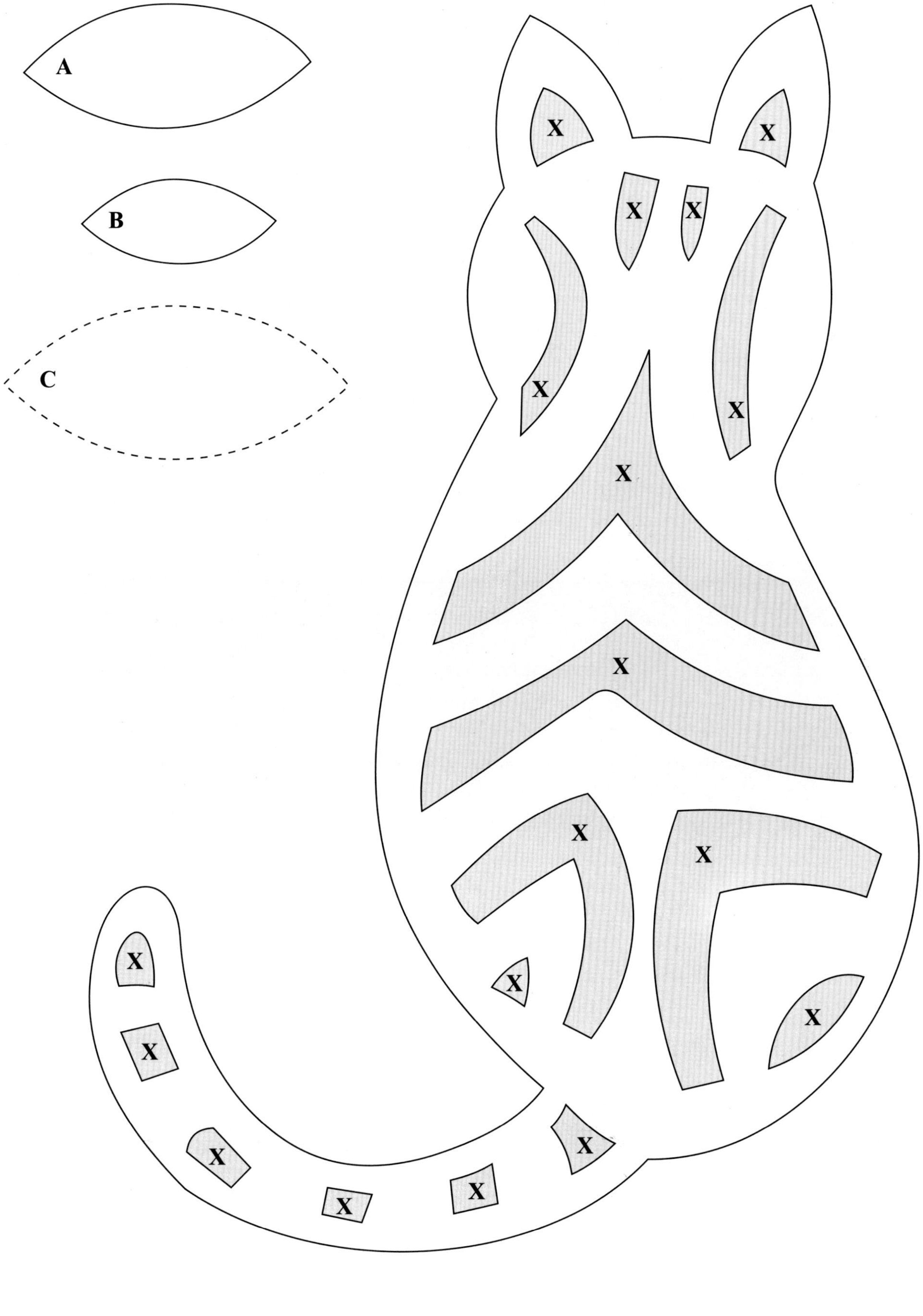
A
B
C
X

Alternative

Ein größerer Wandbehang mit dem Titel „Watching and Waiting" (Beobachten und Warten), bestehend aus vier der beschriebenen Blocks.

Alternative

A larger hanging called "Watching and Waiting" with 4 worked panels as above.

Sommerblumenkissen

Flower Garden Cushion

51 x 51 cm (20" x 20")

Dieses Kissen bringt den Sommergarten ins Haus. Die Blumen können alle im gleichen Farbschema sein, aber auch jede Blume in einer anderen Farbe wäre hübsch. Die Applikationen können von Hand oder mit der Maschine sein.

This is a cushion to bring the summer garden into the house. The flowers may reflect one colour scheme or each could be different. The appliqué may be by hand or by machine.

Stoffbedarf

Heller Druck für die Mitte:
32 x 32 cm (12 1/2" x 12 1/2")
Grün: 1 Quilters Viertel für die Schrägstreifen
Ecken (heller als die Mitte):
25 x 50 cm (10" x 20")
Rot-, Gelb-, Grün-, Brauntöne: Reste
Borte: 15 x 110 cm (6" x 44")
Vliesofix oder Steam-a-Seam: 5 x 8 cm (3" x 2")

Schablonen herstellen.

Schneiden und nähen

Das Mittelquadrat mit einem Raster versehen. Dazu von einer Seite aus gemessen die erste Linie 5,7 cm (2 1/4") von der Kante entfernt aufzeichnen. Die nächsten drei Linien jeweils im Abstand von 5,1 cm (2"). Die letzte Linie sollte wieder 5,7 cm (2 1/4") von der Außenkante entfernt liegen. In die andere Richtung genauso verfahren. Schrägstreifen von 0,6 cm (1/4") fertiger Breite und mindestens 32 cm (12 1/2") Länge nach Ihrer Lieblingsmethode herstellen. Die Streifen auf das Raster reihen, dabei die Streifen an den Kreuzungspunkten einmal über- und einmal untereinander legen, so dass ein regelrechtes Geflecht entsteht. Beidseitig applizieren. Reihfäden entfernen. Die einzelnen Blumenteile können schon miteinander verbunden werden, bevor sie als Ganzes appliziert werden. Die runden Blumenmitten können mit Klebevlies aufgebügelt und mit Knopflochstich festgenäht werden.

Vom Eckstoff 2 Quadrate von 24 cm (9 1/2") schneiden. Diese je einmal diagonal teilen, es entstehen 4 Dreiecke. Das Mittelquadrat auf die Spitze stellen und die Dreiecke annähen. Das neue Quadrat auf 44 cm (17 1/4") zurückschneiden.

Mit Hilfe der Blätterschablone 16 Blätter ausschneiden. Die Blätter so anordnen, dass jeweils 3 in die Ecken ragen und 4 um den Mittelpunkt des Kissens liegen oder in einer beliebigen anderen Anordnung. Applizieren. Blüten darauf platzieren und festnähen.

Fabric requirements

Light print fabric for centre: 12 1/2" square
Green for the trellis bias strips: 1 fat quarter
Lighter print fabric for corner triangles: 10" x 20"
Scraps of coloured fabric for flowers
Scraps of green for leaves
Scraps 3" x 2" for flower centres
Bondaweb: 3" x 2"
Border: 6" x 44"
Binding: 3" x 44"

Make templates.

Method

Mark the centre 12" square by drawing parallel lines from edge to edge 2 1/4" in from one side. Mark 3 more at 2" intervals and the last line 2 1/4" from second side. Turn fabric and repeat drawn lines, giving a 2" grid with 2 1/4" measurements on all 4 sides. Make 1/4" bias strips according to your chosen method, minimum length 12 1/2". Tack the strips centrally to the drawn lines in an over/under basketweave and appliqué each side. Remove all tacking. The flowers can be made individually before being appliquéd to the basketweave background. Using template A, B and C (outer flower, inner flower and centre) cut out flowers making sure a small seam allowance is added if using hand appliqué method. The templates do NOT include a seam allowance. Appliqué the inner flower to the outer flower, then the centre to the whole flower, or alternatively Bondaweb the centre to the middle of the inner flower and blanket stitch to hold. It would also be possible to zig-zag or top stitch this centre in place.

From the corner triangle fabric cut 2 squares 9 1/2" x 9 1/2". Cut both diagonally to make 4 triangles. Place centre trellis square on point and sew 4 corner triangles to each side. Trim new square to 17 1/4" x 17 1/4"
Cut 16 leaves from template.

Appliqué flower and leaf arrangements, one to the middle and one to each of the 4 sides of the trellis. The straight edge of the leaf shapes are placed under the flowers and covered by them. The arrangements can be to your liking and in

Borte

Streifen von 7,5 cm (3") Breite schneiden. Auf der linken Stoffseite der Streifen eine Linie im Abstand von 2,5 cm (1") parallel zur langen Kante markieren.

Jeweils links und rechts des bis dahin fertig gestellten Mittelstücks die Stoffstreifen so unter das Mittelstück legen, dass die Kanten genau auf den markierten Linien liegen. Die Streifen ragen dabei zum größten Teil unter dem Mittelstück hervor. Entlang der Kante des Mittelstücks einreihen. Die Streifen auf die rechte Seite schlagen, so dass sie nun auf dem Mittelstück liegen. Eine Wellenlinie aufzeichnen.

Die Linie sollte jeweils mindestens 0,6 cm (1/4") Abstand zur Reihnaht und zur offenen Kante des Streifens haben. Die Wellenlinie (auf der Seite der Linie, die zur offenen Kante zeigt) nach schneiden. Dabei die Nahtzugabe von 0,6 cm (1/4") nicht vergessen. Die Borte applizieren.

Die anderen beiden Seiten genauso behandeln.

no particular pattern. There are 4 leaves to the middle flower and 3 to each of the four sides.
From the border fabric cut 3" strips across the width. You will need 2 strips 3" x 17 1/4" and 2 strips 3" x 20 3/4". On the reverse of these 3" strips draw a line 1" along the length. On two sides place this 1" marked line along the edge of the marked centre, underneath the central square.

Tack close to centre edge. Turn to right side and draw undulating line, no higher than 1/4" from border top edge and 1/4" from tacking.

Trim wavy edge leaving a 1/4" seam allowance then appliqué border to centre. Repeat for opposite side.

The last two sides are completed in the same way with the undulating wavy line extending across the first two sides.

Quilten

Um alle applizierten Formen herum quilten. Zusätzlich eine Linie parallel zur Wellenlinie in der Borte quilten. Das Kissen nach Ihrer Lieblingsmethode mit einem Reißverschluss oder einem Hotelverschluss fertig stellen. Dabei kann das Kissen verstürzt werden oder, wie hier, wie ein Quilt mit einer Einfassung verschlossen werden.

Alternative

Mit diesen Blumen und dem Gitter kann man einen sehr schönen Quilt nähen. Der hier gezeigte heißt „Sheba's Meadow". Er wurde im Andenken an unsere wunderbare Katze Sheba so betitelt. Sheba wurde 20 Jahre alt und ist in einem kleinen Fleckchen unseres Gartens begraben. Dieses Fleckchen Erde ist zu jeder Jahreszeit mit blühenden Blumen bedeckt.

Quilting

Quilt around all flower shapes, the trellis and appliqué and the wavy border. In addition quilt a single line in the border 1" from the undulating edging and following the undulations.

Complete the cushion by making a back with your preferred fastening. Tack front and back together, wrong sides together and sew on binding all around, as with a quilt. Turn binding over and slip stitch to back of cushion. This gives a 'piped' effect.

Alternative

Even more of these trellis/floral squares plus vines and leaves make a pretty flower quilt. The one pictured is called 'Sheba's Meadow'. We had a wonderful cat called Sheba who lived to be 20. We buried her in a tiny piece of our garden and this area is always covered with flowers in all 4 seasons. We call the plot 'Sheba's Meadow' and this quilt was made in her memory.

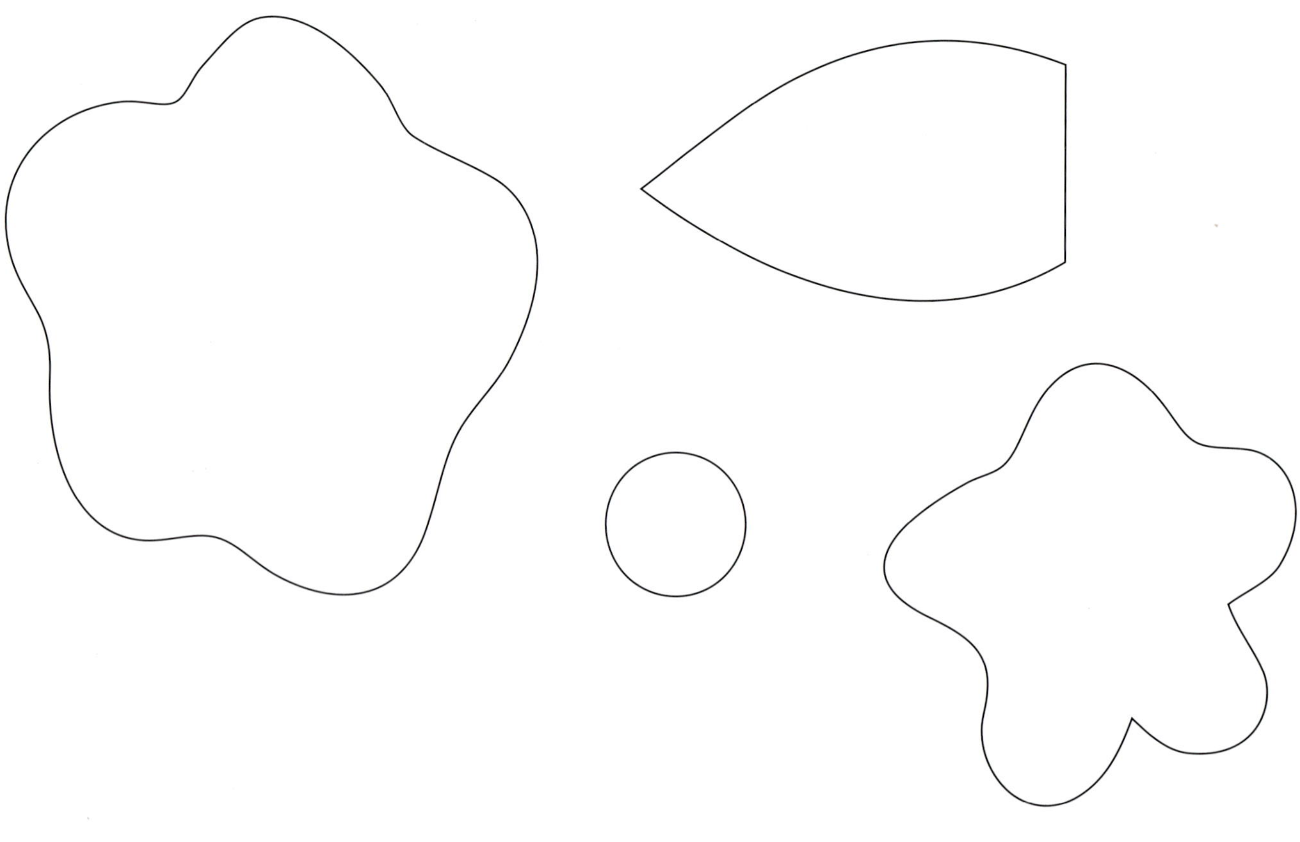

Tulpenfächer

Flower Fan Wallhanging

58,4 x 58,4 cm (23" x 23")

Dieser Entwurf basiert auf dem traditionellen *Großmutters Fächer* Block, allerdings enthält er eingenähte dreidimensionale „Stiele". Applizierte Tulpenblüten am Ende der Stiele und applizierte Blätter auf den Nahtlinien vervollständigen die Blumen.

This design is based on the traditional *Grandmother's Fan* block, with folded fabric inserted in the fan stems. Tulips are appliquéd to the heads of the stems with leaves along the seam line.

Stoffbedarf

Hintergrund: 46 x 110 cm (18″ x 44″)
Ecken: 30 x 110 cm (11″ x 44″)
Stiele, Biesen und Borte: 26 x 110 cm (10″ x 44″)
Blütenblätter: Reste in Rot- und Rosatönen
Blätter: Reste in Grüntönen

Schablonen herstellen.

Schneiden

Hintergrund: Mit der vergrößerten Schablone A 1 Teil, mit Schablone B 4 Teile, 1 Streifen von 31,8 x 7,6 cm (12 1/2 x 3″) und 1 Streifen von 39,4 x 7,6 cm (15 1/2″ x 3″)
Ecken: 2 Quadrate von 27,9 cm (11″), diese je einmal diagonal teilen, es entstehen 4 Dreiecke
Biese und Borte: 2 Streifen von 5,1 x 52,1 cm (2″ x 20 1/2″) und 2 Streifen von 5,1 x 60,7 cm (2″ x 23 1/2″). Den Rest in Streifen von 2,5 cm (1″) Breite, diese jeweils der Länge nach links auf links falten und bügeln
Tulpenblätter: jeweils 5 Stück mit Schablone C und D
Blätter: 12 Stück mit Schablone E

Nähen

Die keilförmigen Fächerteile zusammennähen. Dabei immer einen gefalteten schmalen Stielstreifen dazwischen nähen. Dazu einen gefalteten Streifen rechts auf rechts so auf ein Keilstück legen, dass die offenen Kanten genau auf der langen Kante des Keils liegen. Das nächste Keilstück rechts auf rechts darauf legen. Gut fest stecken und zusammennähen. Mit allen weiteren Stücken genauso verfahren. Den Fächer an das Hintergrundstück A nähen. Dabei sollten die Nähte genau auf die Markierungen des A-Stücks treffen. Zuerst den kürzeren Hintergrundstreifen ansetzen, dann den längeren.
Die Tulpenblätter so auf die Stielenden applizieren, dass sie ungefähr zur Hälfte über die bogige Naht hinausreichen. Mit den Tulpenblättern C anfangen. Das kurze Stück zwischen den Markierungen wird von den Tulpenblättern D verdeckt werden und braucht nicht umgeschlagen werden. Die beiden äußeren Tulpen werden nur durch die Tulpenköpfe und die Blätter angedeutet und haben nur die Naht als Stiel.

Fabric requirements

Background: 18″ x 44″
Corner: 11″ x 44″
Inserts and border: 10″ x 44″
Scraps of pink for 5 tulips
Scraps of green for leaves

Make templates.

Cutting

Background: 1 piece with template A, 4 pieces with template B, 1 piece 12 1/2″ x 3″, 1 piece 15 1/2″ x 3″
Corner: 2 squares of 11″, cut diagonally to give 4 triangles
Border and insert: 2 strips 20 1/2″ x 2″ and 2 strips 23 1/2″ x 2″. Cut remainder into 1″ strips, fold half lengthwise and press.
Pink: 5 pieces from template C and 5 from template D
Green: 12 leaves from template E

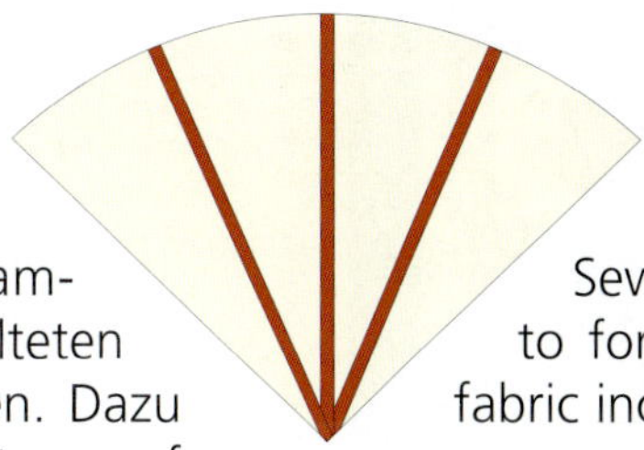

Method

Sew together background wedge shapes to form a fan with lengths of folded insert fabric included in the 3 central seams.

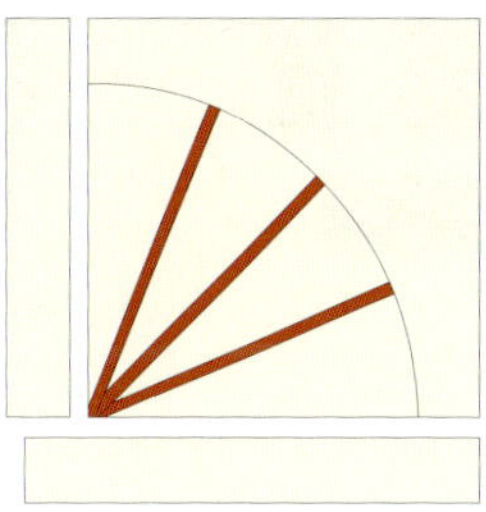

Sew pieced fan to background fabric template A, matching the joins to the notches marked on the template.

Add the short background strip to one side, as shown, then the long strip along the bottom.

Appliqué tulip flowers to top of 'stalks', midway over curved seam. Sew template C pieces first, remembering that the area between the 2 marks will be covered by template D pieces so it is not necessary to turn under that small area on the C pieces. Appliqué the leaves in positions where the last 2 stems are (the outside ones without the folded inserts) and then just below the flowers. See photograph of completed wallhanging for reference.

Das fertige Mittelstück auf die Spitze stellen und die Eckdreiecke zusammen mit den übrigen Biesen annähen. Die Bortenstreifen zuerst seitlich, dann oben und unten ansetzen.

Quilten

Die Tulpenschablonen können auch gut zum Markieren eines Quiltmusters genutzt werden. Besonders in den Ecken kann man Tulpenköpfe quilten. Innerhalb des Mittelstücks quiltet man besser einige gerade Linien, um das Fächerdesign zu betonen.

Place centre piece on point, add 4 corner triangles, inserting folded fabric lengths into seams. Add border strips to sides, then top and bottom.

Quilting

The tulip and leaves templates can be used to quilt the 4 corner triangles. Within this central area, quilt straight lines to accentuate the fan design.

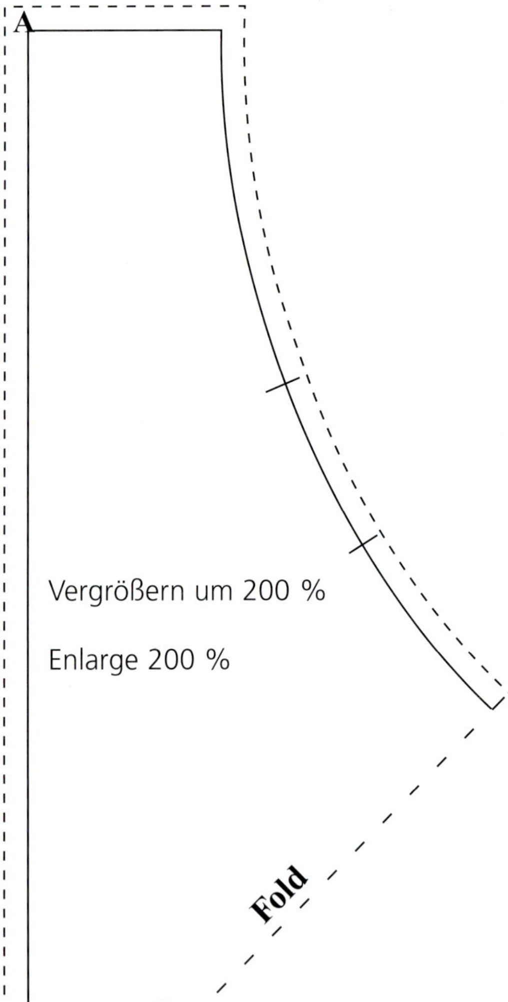

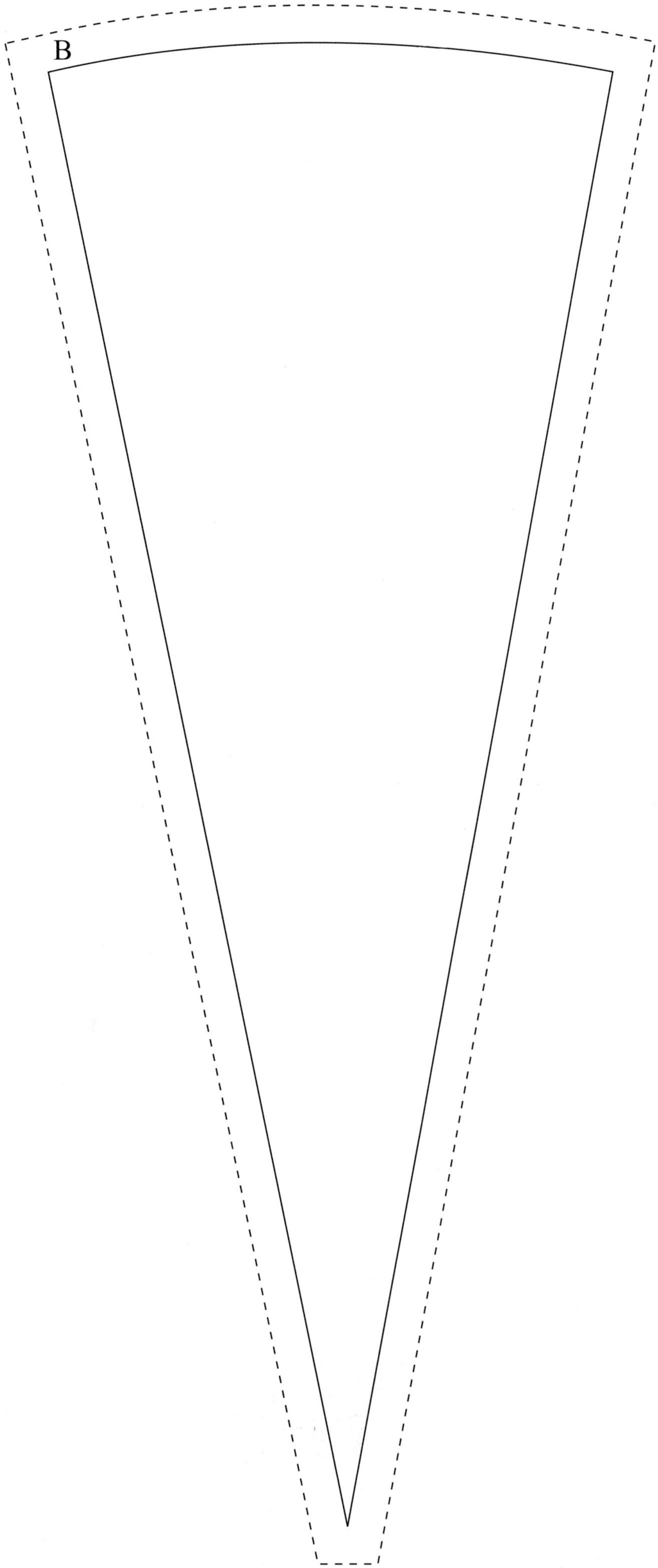
B

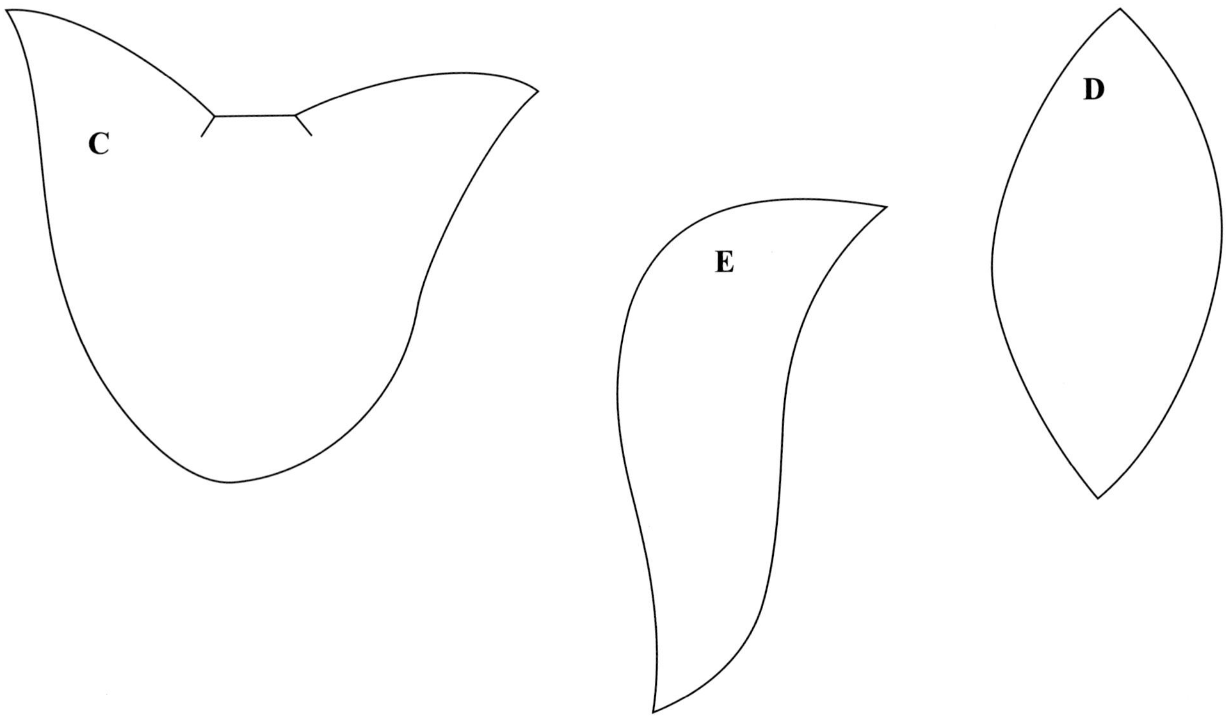
C
E
D

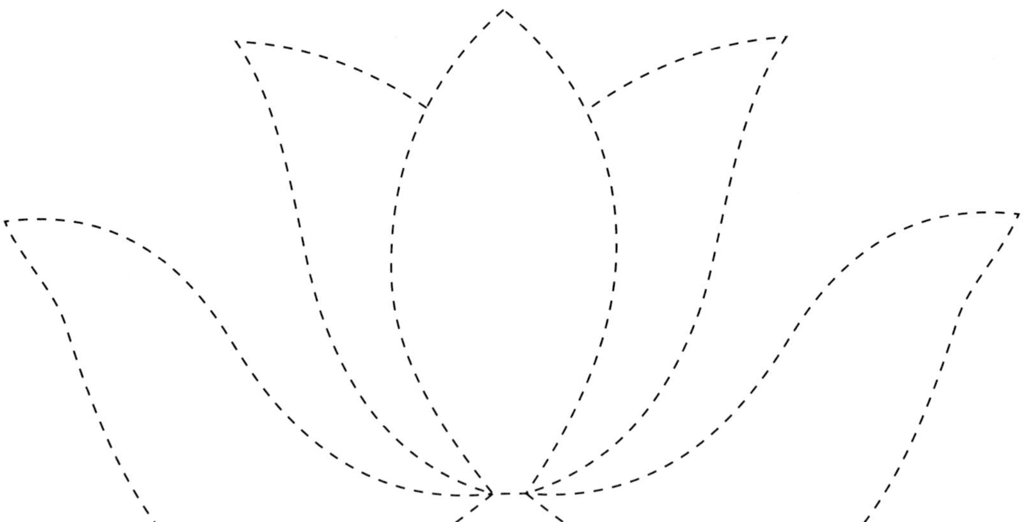

Alternative

Für einen großen Quilt kann man die Stiele mit verschiedenen Blütenköpfen versehen und so unterschiedliche Blocks herstellen. Diese kann man auf verschiedene Weise arrangieren, ob im geraden oder diagonalen Raster oder in Gruppen wie in unserem Beispiel.

Alternative

By using different flowers and leaves other blocks can be made and featured in a bed quilt. The blocks would be made on exactly the same basis as the tulips. They could be arranged in many different ways or in groups as in the picture.

39 x 42 cm (15 1/2" x 16 1/2")

Tasche mit keltischem Design

Wählen Sie kräftige Farben und diese Tasche wird ein echter Hingucker. Hierbei lernen Sie, wie man aus einfachen Formen und entsprechendem Arrangement fließende keltische Designs zaubert.

Celtic Floral Tote Bag

Choose bright colours for this eye-catching tote bag. Learn how to make Celtic border patterns from simple shapes, which when placed end-to-end make flowing Celtic designs.

Stoffbedarf

Mittelstreifen: 11,5 x 81,5 cm (4 1/2" x 32")
Seitenstreifen, (jeweils 2 farblich zueinander passende Streifen, insgesamt 4): 9 x 81,5 cm (3 1/2" x 32")
Schrägstreifen (3 verschiedene Stoffe, die farblich harmonieren): jeweils ein Quilters Viertel
Futter: 81,5 x 42 cm (32" x 16 1/2")
Griffe: 2 Streifen von 7,5 x 45,5 cm (3" x 18")
Vlies: 46 x 86,5 cm (18" x 34")

Schablonen herstellen.

Schneiden und nähen

Den Mittelstreifen einmal der Länge nach in die Hälfte falten, um die Mitte zu markieren. Schauen Sie sich das keltische Muster gut an. Mit Schablone A anfangen. Diese an einem Ende des Mittelstreifens der Länge nach genau auf die Mittellinie platzieren. Mit Bleistift Konturen markieren. Schablone B exakt in die Mitte dieser Markierung legen und die Konturen markieren. Schablone A mit einer Spitze an das soeben markierte kleine Oval legen, ebenfalls exakt auf der Mittellinie. Mit Bleistift Kontur markieren. Schablone B wieder in die Mitte legen, die Spitze sollte an die Spitze des zuerst markierten Ovals A stoßen, markieren. So im Wechsel fortfahren bis der gesamte Streifen markiert ist. Die Bleistiftlinien werden später durch die Schrägstreifen verdeckt.

Schrägstreifen aus zwei verschiedenen Stoffen herstellen. Mit einer Farbe anfangen. Den Schrägstreifen genau auf die Bleistiftlinien legen und einreihen. Dabei an den Kreuzungspunkten offenlassen, damit der zweite Schrägstreifen unter Umständen unter dem ersten durchgeführt werden kann. Den zweiten Schrägstreifen auflegen und einreihen. Immer an den Kreuzungspunkten die Streifen miteinander verweben, das heißt einmal untereinander, bei der nächsten Kreuzung übereinander führen.

Jeweils zwei Seitenstreifen der Länge nach zusammennähen. Die Nahtlinie dient als Orientierungslinie für Schablone C. Wie beim Mittelstreifen Schablone C entlang der Nahtlinie auflegen und die Kontur markieren. So fortfah-

Fabric requirements

Centre panel: 4 1/2" x 32"
Side panel: 2 co-ordinating fabrics each 3 1/2" x 32"
Bias tape: 3 fabrics 12" each. Joining strips where necessary to make required length.
Lining: 32" x 16 1/2"
Handles: 2 strips 18" x 3"
Wadding: 34" x 18"

Make templates.

Method

Fold central panel lengthwise to show central line. Take templates A and B and study the pattern attached. Place template A at the beginning, centralizing the template on the central line. Draw round template with a pencil. Take template B and place centrally as before, joining first marked template A, draw round with a pencil. Continue alternating A and B along length of panel. Using template B place centrally within first marked template A, then take A and again join onto template B just marked. Continue along length of panel, alternating A and B as before. At the top and bottom of the panel there will be a partial template to complete the lines. All pencil marks will be hidden by bias in due course.

Make the bias from 2 of the bias fabrics using your preferred method. Start with one of them, centring on one of the marked lines and tack, then sew on each side interlacing 'over' and 'under'. With the same colour, tack and sew again the reverse Celtic line. See attached pattern and pictured tote bag for guidance. Repeat with 2nd contrast bias fabric for remaining marked lines.

For each side panel sew together lengthwise one of each fabric. This sewn line now acts as a guide for placing template C centrally. Start at the bottom and mark round template C, then move template up as before. This is an easier arrangement. The third bias fabric is used on these side panels and the bias will sometimes be sewn on one of the side panels and then on the other.

ren bis die Streifen vollständig markiert sind. Den Schrägstreifen auflegen, einreihen und beidseitig applizieren.

Vom Vlies 2 Streifen von 2,5 x 46 cm (1″ x 18″) abschneiden für die Griffe.

Den Mittelstreifen genau auf die Mitte des verbliebenen Vliesstücks platzieren und feststecken. Jeweils links und rechts die Seitenstreifen annähen. Dazu einen Seitenstreifen rechts auf rechts auf den Mittelstreifen legen und durch das Vlies hindurch annähen. Aufklappen. Mit dem zweiten Streifen genauso verfahren. Entlang des keltischen Musters quilten. Nur durch das Oberteil und das Vlies. Nach dem Quilten das Vlies an den langen Seiten genau bis an den Stoff zurückschneiden. An den kurzen Seiten jeweils 2,5 cm (1″) Überstand stehen lassen. Das Futter genau auf das Maß des Stoffes schneiden. Das überstehende Vlies dabei nicht berücksichtigen. Das Futter und das gequiltete Stück jeweils separat einmal rechts auf rechts quer in die Hälfte falten. Die beiden gefalteten Teile genau aufeinander legen, bei beiden sieht man die linke Seite. Die Seitennähte schließen. Man erhält zwei miteinander verbundene Taschen oder Fächer. An der gefalteten Bodenseite die beiden Teile jeweils so auseinanderzupfen, dass man die Ecken wie in der Abbildung aufeinander legen kann. Etwa 2,5 cm (1″) von der entstandenen Spitze entfernt quer nähen. In die Tasche, die die Außenseite bilden soll hineingreifen und sie wie einen Kissenbezug über die Futtertasche stülpen.

Griffe herstellen

Dazu die Vliesstreifen jeweils auf die linke Seite der Stoffstreifen in der Mitte platzieren. Den Stoff der Länge nach von beiden Seiten darüber falten. Eine Seite etwa 0,6 cm (1/4″) einschlagen und die offene Kante damit überdecken. Mit der Maschine absteppen. Die Griffe jeweils etwa 10 cm von den Kanten entfernt auf der Schauseite der Tasche platzieren. Feststecken. Den Umfang der Taschenöffnung ausmessen. Einen Stoffstreifen in dieser Länge plus einer Zugabe von 1,5 cm (1/2″) und einer Breite von 6,5 cm

Cut 2 strips 1″ wide from 18″ measurement of wadding, giving two strips of wadding 1″ x 18″ and reserve for handles

Place the central panel in the middle of the remaining piece of wadding and tack in place. Join each side panel by placing right sides together and sewing through fabric and wadding with a 1/4″ seam. Turn side pieces over and tack all round.

Quilt round both sides of all the Celtic appliqué with just the top and wadding – no lining. After quilting trim the wadding exactly to the long sides of the piece but leave 1″ at each end. Cut lining to exactly the same size as the worked piece – do not include the 1″ wadding extension.

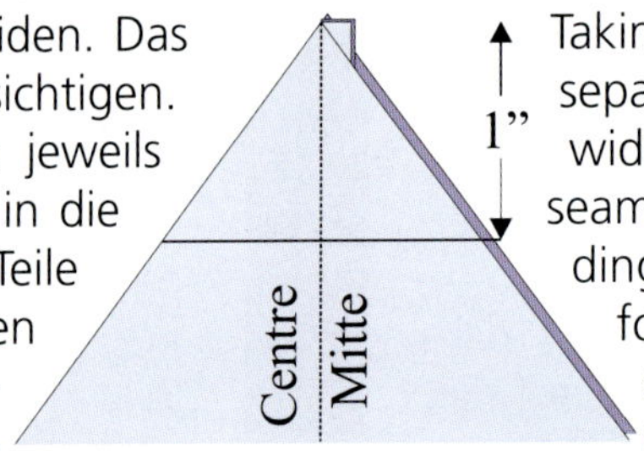

Taking the worked piece and the lining, separately fold in half, right sides together, widthwise and sew side seams with a 1/4″ seam, treating the worked piece and wadding as one whole. On the wrong side, fold bottom corners to form a point and sew edge to edge to 1″ in from point. Repeat on all lower corners of main piece and on lining – this will form a base for the tote bag.

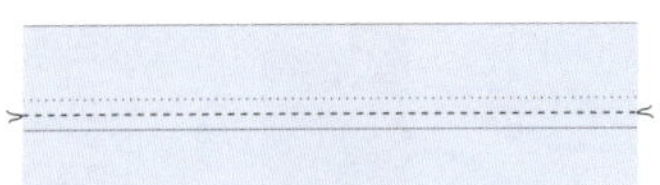

Insert lining into worked piece wrong sides together and tack all round top.

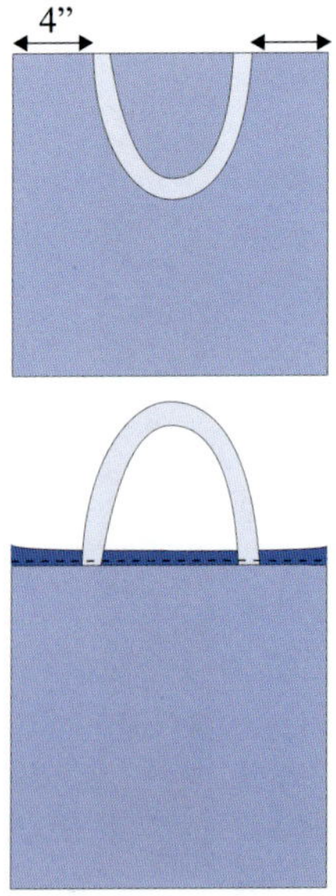

Handles

The handles can be made from any of the bias strip fabrics which are left over, but any other additional toning fabric may be used. Cut 2 pieces 2″ x 18″. Place wadding strips cut earlier in the centre lengthwise. Fold edges to middle enclosing wadding, turn one edge over 1/4″ and overlap second edge. Stitch down centre.
Place handles 4″ from each side of main bag and tack in place.

Again, using left over fabrics from the bias fabrics – joining if necessary – cut a piece

(2 1/2") schneiden ca. 6,5 x 79,5 cm (2 1/2" x 31 1/2"). Die kurzen Enden zusammennähen. Mit der rechten Seite auf die offene Kante der Schauseite legen, feststecken und rundherum annähen. Dabei die Griffe mit festnähen. Den Streifen über die offene Kante ins Innere der Tasche falten, die offene Kante des Streifens dabei 0,6 cm (1/4") einschlagen, feststecken und mit der Maschine von der Schauseite aus festnähen. Dabei darauf achten, dass die Griffe nach oben zeigen. Die Griffe an der Oberkante der Tasche nochmals festnähen.

2 1/2" x measurement all round the top of the bag (approx. 31") plus 1/2" for overlapping. Join ends together.

Sew right sides together all round top of the bag, enclosing the ends of the handles also. Turn edging over to the inside of the bag, turn under 1/4" to secure raw edge and tack in place. On right side, sew on this line of tacking, making sure the handles are upright.
Further secure handles by sewing a line where they cross the top edging of the bag.

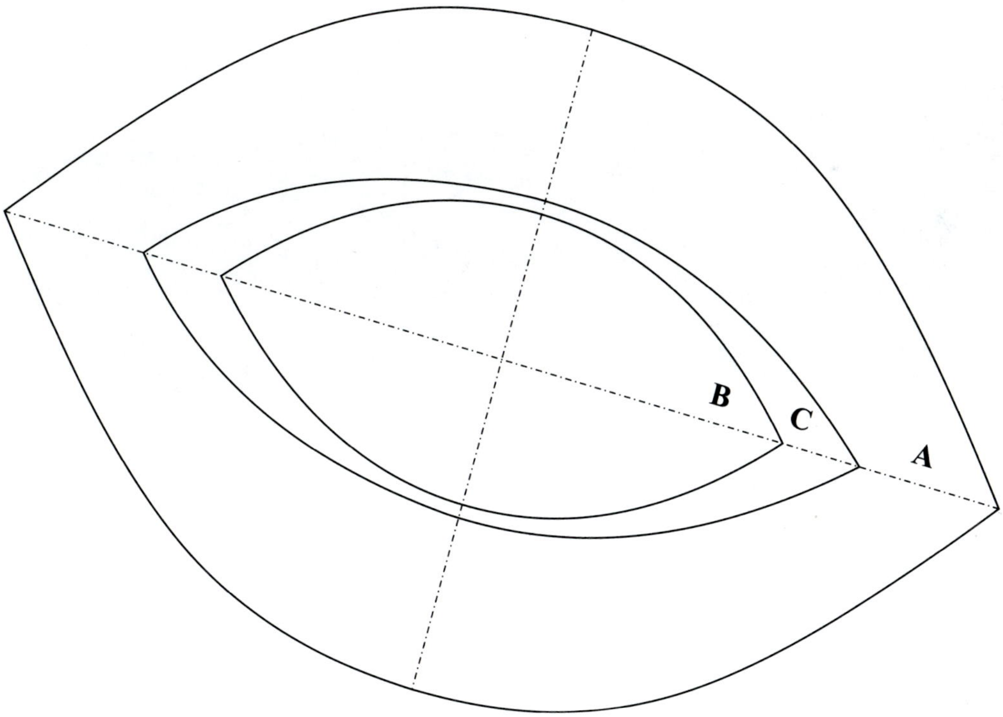

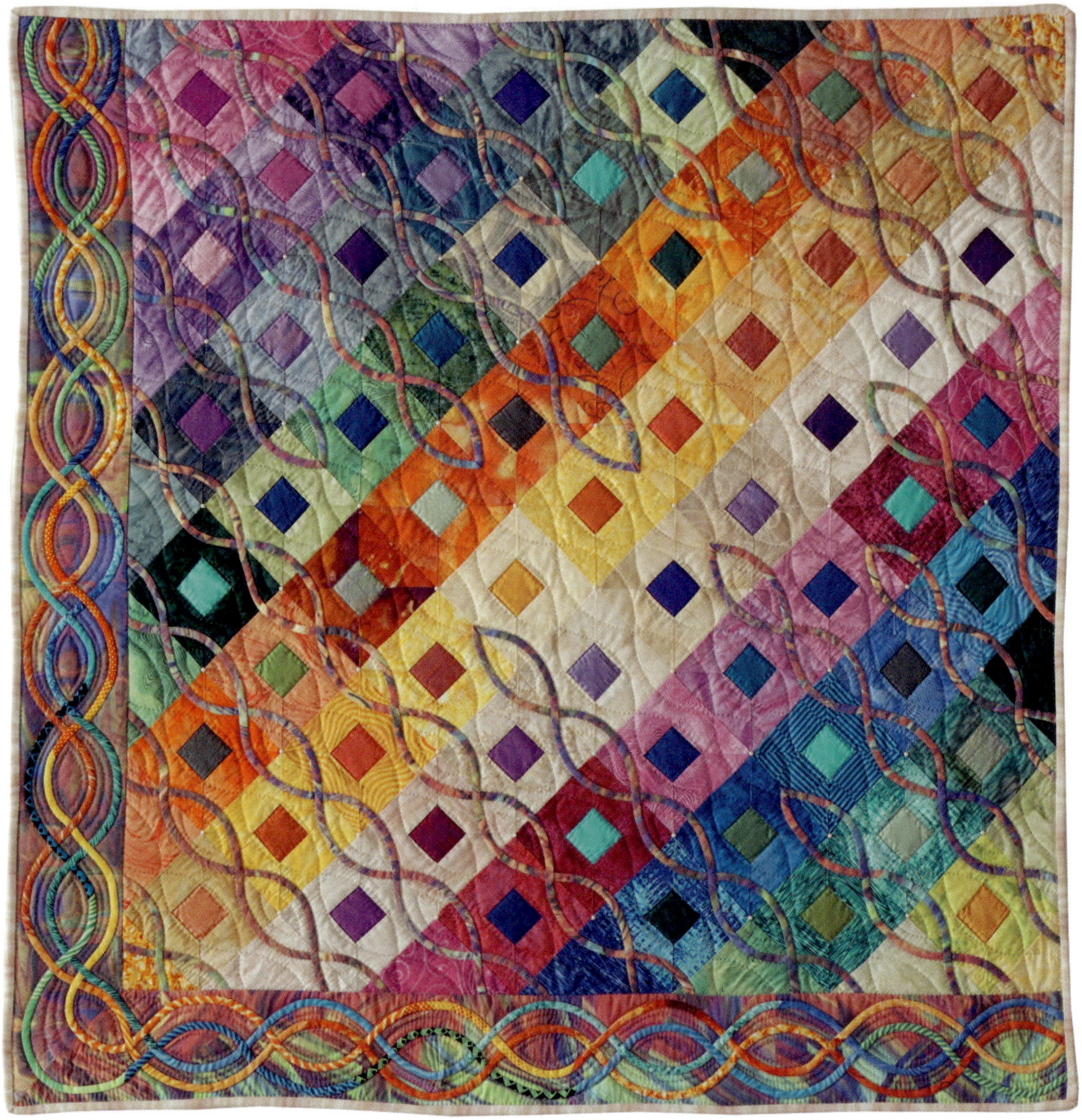

Alternative

Diesen Quilt nenne ich Malkasten, da mich die kleinen Blocks an die bunten Quadrate eines Malkastens erinnerten. Nur zwei Seiten haben eine Borte, die dasselbe keltische Muster hat wie die Tasche. Aber die Schrägstreifen bestehen aus vielen verschiedenen Stoffen unterschiedlicher Länge. Das einfachere keltische Muster ist diagonal über den ganzen Quilt angeordnet.

Alternative

This wall quilt is called 'Paintbox' as the centre squares of the small blocks reminded me of the coloured squares in paintboxes. Only 2 of the sides have borders and the Celtic pattern is the same as the centre panel in the tote bag, but many different fabrics in different lengths are included in the bias strips. The second simpler bias design is used diagonally across the quilt.

40,5 x 110 cm (16" x 44")

Spiel mit Blocks Tischläufer

Dies ist eine interessante Übung für das Arrangieren von Blocks. Nehmen Sie einen einfachen Block, hier Birds in the Air (Vögel im Flug), dessen Grundeinheit auf unterschiedlichste Weise zusammengesetzt werden kann und so immer neue Muster bildet. Das fertige Resultat kann entweder als einfache Patchworkarbeit genutzt werden oder noch mit so genanntem Broderie Perse (persische Applikation) verziert werden. Hierbei werden fertige Motive aus einem Stoff ausgeschnitten (mit kleiner Nahtzugabe) und auf den Hintergrund appliziert.

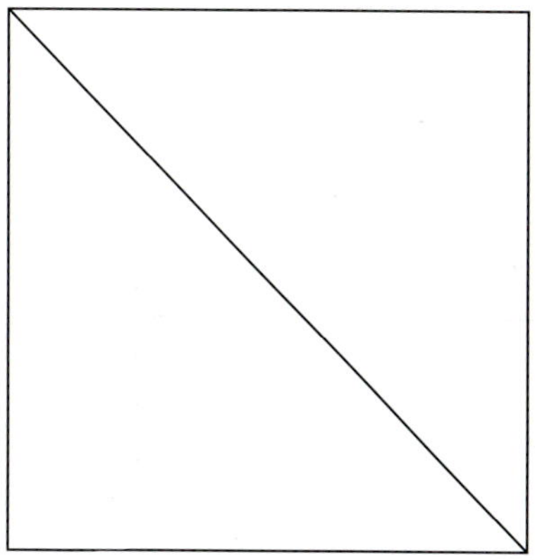

Block Play Table Runner

This is an interesting exercise in block arrangements. Use a simple block, in this case *Birds in the Air,* which can be joined together in many different ways – see the print out of suggestions which will also show the arrangements used in this table runner. The final result can either be used as a pieced project or it can also be enhanced with additional broderie perse – yet another form of appliqué where motifs from a print fabric can be cut out with a small seam, then appliquéd to the main work. Firstly the instructions for the pieced table runner.

Stoffbedarf

Bei einer Stoffbreite von 110 cm (44"):
Hintergrund: 50 cm (20")
Kontrastfarbe 1: 30 cm (12")
Kontrastfarbe 2 (inklusive Einfassung):
40 cm (16")

Schablone herstellen. Schablone B dient zur Überprüfung der Quadrate.

Pro Block schneiden

Hintergrund: 12 Quadrate von 7,3 cm (2 7/8"), 2 Quadrate von 9,9 cm (3 7/8"), diese beiden je einmal diagonal teilen, 4 Streifen von 5 x 32 cm (2" x 12 1/2")
Je Kontrastfarbe: 3 Quadrate von 7,3 cm (2 7/8") und 2 Stücke mit der Schablone

Nähen

Immer ein Hintergrundquadrat und ein Kontrastquadrat rechts auf rechts legen. Eine Diagonale markieren und jeweils links und rechts davon im Abstand von 0,6 cm (1/4") nähen. Auf der Diagonalen schneiden. Bügeln. Die einzelnen Teile wie in der Abbildung zusammensetzen. Verschiedene Blockarrangements nähen. Drei Blocks mit Trennstreifen miteinander verbinden, dabei auch oben und unten je einen Trennstreifen ansetzen. Die Länge des Tischläufers ausmessen, 2 Streifen in dieser Länge und 5 cm (2") Breite schneiden und jeweils links und rechts ansetzen. Wer möchte, kann dieses Oberteil noch mit applizierten Blüten verzieren. Dazu geeignete gedruckte Motive aus einem Stoff ausschneiden und applizieren. Wie üblich einreihen und quilten. Hier wurde mit der Maschine 0,6 cm (1/4") von den Nähten entfernt gequiltet.

Fabric requirements

Background: 50 cm (20")
1st Contrast: 30 cm (12")
2nd Contrast: 40 cm (16") (to include binding)

Make templates. Checking template B is to confirm accuracy of squares.

Fabric will be cut in strips across width.

Cutting per block

Background: 4 strips of 2" width, set aside for sashing. 1 strip of 2 7/8" width, cut this into squares. Of these squares cut 6 diagonally into 12 triangles. Take the other 6 squares and mark diagonal lines on reverse side. Cut one more strip 3 7/8" across width, then cut into squares and lastly diagonally into triangles.
From both contrast fabrics: cut 1 strip 2 7/8" wide. Cut into squares.
Using both contrast fabrics again, cut two shapes from template A, which includes seam allowance of 1/4".
Take 1 background square and one contrast square. Place right sides together with the background fabric on top. Sew 1/4" either side of marked line and cut on the line, making two half-square triangle squares. Repeat twice with same contrast fabric and 3 times with second contrast fabric.
To make one quarter of a block (6" finished square) take 1 half triangle square with first contrast fabric, 2 half-triangle squares with second contrast fabric and 3 background triangles. For the second half of this quarter block join template piece in first contrast fabric (i. e. the same as top left hand half-square triangle square) with one 3 7/8" background triangle.

Join the two pieced triangles to make one 6" (finished) square.
Make second 6" square, reversing contrast fabrics colour – wise.
Make 2 more 6" blocks as first 2.
Study block arrangements and select 3.
Assemble blocks with sashing strips cut to size.
Sew the remaining 2" strips to each long side.
Complete the table runner with backing, wadding, quilting design and binding with second contrast colour.

Alternative

Ein großer Wandbehang mit dem Titel Muschelsucher. Der Hauptstoff hat einen Muscheldruck, der zu den applizierten Seesternen und dem Seetang inspirierte. Die Muschelborte ist revers appliziert. Vier verschiedene Arrangements des Birds in the Air Blocks bilden den Hauptteil des Quilts, der mit Broderie Perse Muscheln, die aus dem Hauptstoff geschnitten wurden, verziert ist.

Alternative

A large wall quilt is shown called 'Shellseekers'. The main fabric featured a shell print, which inspired the seaweed and starfish appliqué with the reverse appliqué shell border.
Four arrangements of the 'Birds in the Air' block as featured in the table runner and the broderie perse element is the addition of shell shapes cut from the main fabric print.

Vier Jahreszeiten Tischsets

Four Seasons Place Mats

30 x 40,5 cm (12" x 16")

Ein Tischset für jede Jahreszeit, jedes mit einer zur Jahreszeit passenden applizierten Blüte und in der Farbe der Saison. Der Hauptteil jedes kleinen Quilts ist mit applizierten Kreisen aus Schrägstreifen verziert, die uns daran erinnern, dass jede Jahreszeit immer wieder kommt.

A placemat for each season of the year, each one with appliqué flowers and made with colours to suit the time of year. The main section of each mat has appliqué bias circles intertwined, reminding us that the seasons come round every year

Stoffbedarf pro Set

Hintergrund Hauptteil: 30 x 30 cm (12" x 12")
Seitenteil: 11,5 x 35,5 cm
Blüten: Reste in passenden Farben für Tulpen, Rosen, Astern und Christrosen

Schablonen herstellen.

Schneiden und nähen, Seitenteil

Den Streifen für das Seitenteil auf 11,5 x 30 cm (4 1/2 x 12") kürzen. Den Rest aufbewahren. Den Streifen einmal der Länge nach und einmal quer falten, um den Mittelpunkt zu bestimmen. Hierauf Kreisschablone A zentrieren und Kontur nachzeichnen. Jeweils einen Kreis oberhalb und unterhalb so aufzeichnen, dass sich die Kreise fast berühren. Dies ergibt ein keltisches Muster. Dafür wird ein Schrägstreifen von mindestens 89 cm (35") Länge benötigt. Das Grün sollte der Jahreszeit angepasst sein. An einem Kreuzungspunkt beginnen und den Schrägstreifen rundherum applizieren, dabei den Schrägstreifen an den Kreuzungspunkten einmal oben und einmal unten kreuzen lassen. Der Anfangspunkt sollte unbedingt unten liegen und durch den kreuzenden Streifen verdeckt werden. Die zur Jahreszeit passende Blume innerhalb der Kreise platzieren und applizieren.

Schneiden und nähen, Hauptteil

Kreisschablonen B, C und D auf jedem Hauptteil anders anordnen. Sie sollten überlappen. Auf jedem Hintergrund sind vier Kreise, aber Kreis B sollte überall nur einmal vorkommen. Für Kreis B wird ein Schrägstreifen von mindestens 51 cm (20") Länge gebraucht, für Kreis C mindestens 41 cm (16") und Kreis D mindestens 25,5 cm (10"). Die Farben der Schrägstreifen zur entsprechenden Jahreszeit passend wählen. Immer an einem Kreuzungspunkt beginnen, damit Anfang und Ende durch einen kreuzenden Schrägstreifen verdeckt werden.

Wer möchte, kann nun zusätzlich den Namen der Jahreszeit applizieren. Dazu wie folgt vorgehen. Auf den abgeschnittenen Rest des Seitenteils den Jahreszeitennamen übertragen. Das geht am einfachsten mit Hilfe einer Lichtbox

Fabric requirements for each mat

Main part: 12" x 12"
Side of main part and optional name of season: 4 1/2" x 14"
Lengths of cut bias as noted in main instructions.
Scraps of fabric in colours suitable for tulips, roses, asters and Christmas roses.

Make templates.

Method

Cut side strip fabric to 4 1/2" x 12" and reserve remaining scrap for later.

Find centre of side strip by folding lengthwise, then width wise. Place circle template A centrally and draw round on fabric. Draw 2 more circles, one above and one below the central circle, almost but not quite touching. This now makes a Celtic pattern. You will need at least 35" of folded bias in a green shade to match the season you are working on. Start at the 'crossing' point of two of the circles and appliqué the bias all round, the Celtic pattern weaving under and over, noting that the starting point will be an 'under' and therefore hiding the starting and ending point of the bias. The seasonal flower can now be appliquéd in the centre of each circle and detailed instructions for each flower follow later.

Take the main fabric and place circle shapes B, C and D in an arrangement of your own design making sure they are linked by overlaying one shape over another. You will need 4 circle shapes in total but use circle B only once. You will see from the picture illustrating the mats that 4 different circle arrangements have been used. For circle B you will need a folded bias strip of at least 20", for circle C at least 16" and circle D at least 10". For these bias strips use fabric colours connected to the relevant season. Start at one overlaying point on one of the circles and appliqué right size folded bias strip all round the circle, again an under/over succession as you meet the other drawn circles. This enables the start and finish of each bias strip to be hidden. Complete the other 3 circles the same way, starting each bias strip at an 'under' point.

oder man klebt das Muster direkt auf die Fensterscheibe, damit die Vorlage durch den Stoff scheint und abgepaust werden kann. Mit einem Stielstich, einem kleinen Kettstich oder einem anderen Zierstich nachsticken, dazu Stickgarn verwenden. Die entsprechende Kreisschablone auf die linke Stoffseite so platzieren, dass die Stickerei genau hineinpasst, Kontur nachzeichnen. Auf der Linie ausschneiden. Mit Hilfe eines Schrägstreifens, der die offenen Kanten verdeckt, applizieren. Da es hier keinen Kreuzungspunkt gibt, an dem Anfang und Ende versteckt werden können, muss der Streifen vorher zum Kreis geschlossen werden. Dazu einen Schrägstreifen von 16,5 cm (6 1/2") Länge schneiden. Die Nahtzugaben von 0,6 cm (1/4") an den kurzen Enden markieren und zusammennähen. Jetzt erst den Streifen wie üblich falten, über die Kreiskontur legen, dieser Kreis sollte irgendwo innerhalb des Kreises B liegen, einreihen und applizieren.

Seitenteil und Hauptteil miteinander verbinden und wie üblich einreihen und außerhalb und innerhalb aller Kreise quilten. Nach dem Quilten zusätzlich noch eine Rückwand anfügen, damit die Tischsets stabiler werden. Die Rückwand kann zusammen mit den Einfassungsstreifen angenäht werden.

Frühling: Tulpe

Teil 1 und 2 sollten aus zwei verschiedenen Stoffen bestehen. Zuerst Teil 1 applizieren. Die kleine Stelle zwischen den Markierungen sollte eine Nahtzugabe von 0,6 cm (1/4") haben und offen bleiben. Teil 2 genau darüber platzieren und festnähen. Insgesamt werden 3 Tulpen gebraucht.

Sommer: Rose

Schablonen für Teile 1 und 3 herstellen, Stoffe in zwei verschiedenen Farben damit ausschneiden. Teil 2 ist ein Quadrat von 4,5 cm (1 3/4") und kann mit Hilfe des Lineals zugeschnitten werden. Das Quadrat sollte eine dritte Farbe haben. Das Quadrat einmal links auf links in die Hälfte falten, dann zu einem Dreieck.
Zuerst Teil 1 applizieren, den geraden Teil mit einer Nahtzugabe von 0,6 cm (1/4") offen las-

Join the main part and the side strip together and you will have a mat shape measuring 15 1/2 x 11 1/2. NB see note below. Sandwich and quilt as usual.

NB Note: at this point you can add the seasonal name as follows, but this is an optional extra. Cut a template for the *Season's Name Circle.* Take the reserved piece of fabric the same colour as the side strip. Place this on top of the relevant Season's name and if the fabric is light enough it should be possible to trace the name onto the fabric. If not you can use a light box or even tape to a window to see the words underneath. Using embroidery floss, embroider the name of the season, using stem stitch, a small chain stitch (as used in the samples) or a stitch of your choice. Turn piece to the back, place the Name Circle template on top of the stitching and draw round the circle. Cut out on the line. This also has to be appliquéd to the mat with a folded bias strip to cover the raw edge of the circle but this time there is no 'under' point to hide the edges of the bias so it must be joined prior to appliqué. Cut a bias strip 6 1/2" long, mark a seam line 1/4" in from each end and note that the 45° ends are pointing the same way.

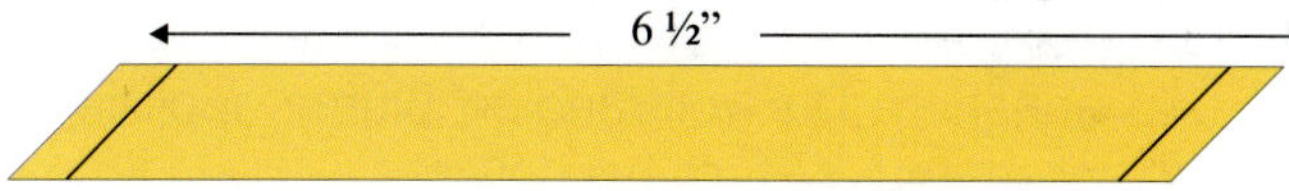

Form a circle by joining the two ends on the seam line, then fold the strip using the method outlined in the initial 'how to' chapter at the beginning of the book. Tack the Season's name piece on the mat, somewhere within large circle B, not necessarily central, and then sew down bias circle to cover raw edges.

Flowers

For spring the theme is a tulip, for summer a rose, for autumn an aster and for winter a Christmas rose. To make each flower follow the directions below.

Spring – Tulip

Make templates of the two parts and cut from two different fabrics with 1/8" seam allowance, apart from central marked top of first piece

sen. Das gefaltete Dreieck darauf platzieren, feststecken und zusammen mit Teil 3 festnähen. 3 Rosen herstellen.

Herbst: Aster

Im Grunde ist die Aster ein Yoyo. Kreis ausschneiden und knappkantig einreihen. Faden fest anziehen, so dass ein kleines Säckchen entsteht. Flach drücken. Kleinen Kreis ausschneiden und mit Klebevlies genau auf die Öffnung kleben. Mit Knopflochstich festnähen.
Komplette Aster applizieren. 3 Astern werden gebraucht.

Winter: Christrose

Schablonen herstellen. Teil 1 aus weißem Stoff mit einer Nahtzugabe von 0,3 cm (1/8") ausschneiden. Teil 2 aus gelbem Stoff genau auf der Linie ausschneiden. Aus Teil 2 ein kleines Yoyo herstellen, wie bei der Aster beschrieben. Die Öffnung aber nach unten direkt auf Teil 1 legen und annähen. Die vollständige Blume applizieren. Insgesamt 3 Stück herstellen.

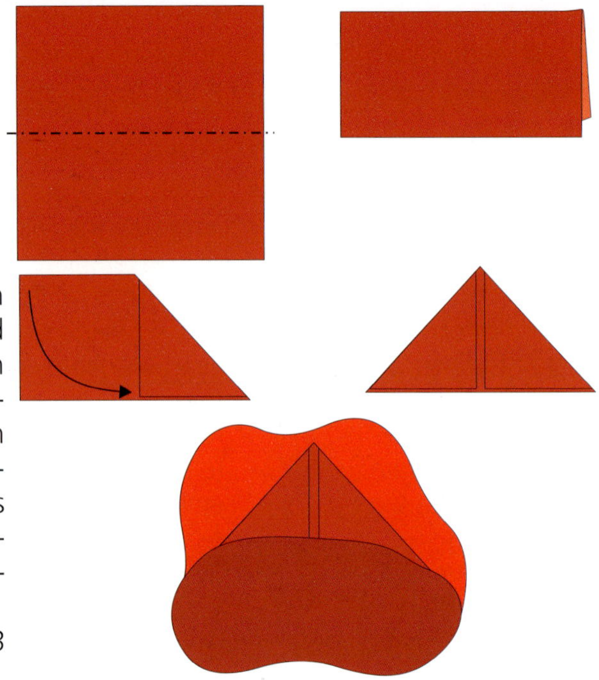

where second part overlaps. This central piece should be 1/4" seam allowance. Appliqué part 1 first, centrally onto one of the Celtic circle patterns, then appliqué the 2nd to make the whole flower. Make 3 tulips in total.

Summer – Rose

Make templates of shapes 1 and 3 in two different fabrics and a square 1 3/4" x 1 3/4" (2) in third fabric. Fold this square in half, then top right and top left to centre bottom.

Cut out shapes 1 and 3 with 1/8" seam allowance, except straight edge of shape 1 which should be 1/4".
Appliqué shape 1 centrally onto one of Celtic circles. Place folded shape 2 on top, then shape 3 to make whole rose (shown below). Make 3 roses in total.

The side edges of the folded shape 2 should be sewn down but central folds left open.

Autumn – Aster

Make template of Aster Circle. Sew running stitch all round edge and gather up, tying tightly.

Make a template for the Aster centre. Cut fabric to exact size of centre and use Bondaweb or other adhesive means to place in middle onto raw edges of gathered aster. Secure with blanket stitch to hold in place. Appliqué whole flower centrally on to Celtic circle pattern. Make 3 Asters in total.

Winter – Christmas Rose

Make templates 1 and 2 – cut shape 1 from white fabric with 1/8" seam and shape 2 from yellow exactly on line. Tack all round yellow circle shape and gather up, as with aster flowers, but this time place raw edges of gathering face down in the middle of the white flower. Slip

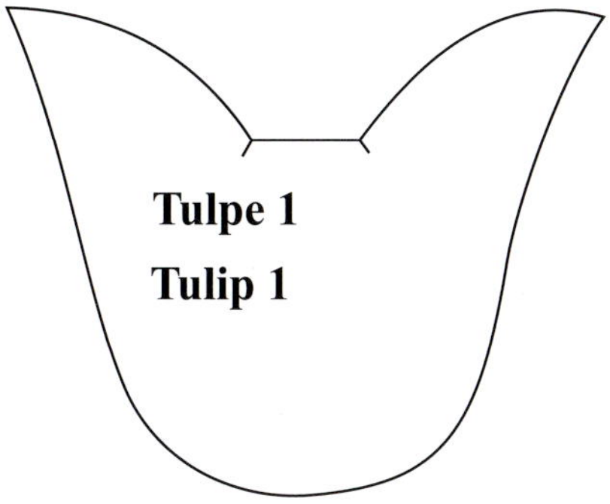

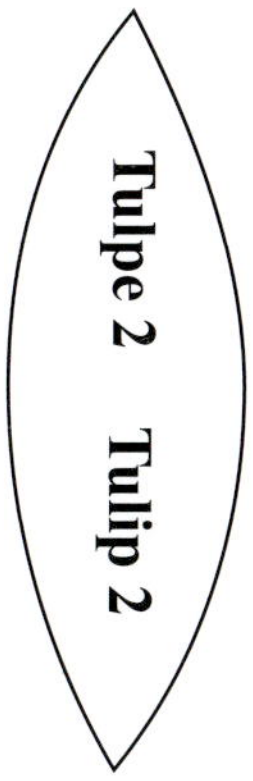

stitch in place then appliqué whole flower centrally onto Celtic circle pattern. Make 3 Christmas Roses in total.

Quilting

Quilt round both sides of all the circle shapes, the Celtic appliqué and all round the flowers. Now place the whole quilted mat onto an 18″ x 14″ backing fabric. The combination of a lining plus a backing makes the place mats stronger.
Tack round edges to hold in place. Machine quilt on the line joining the two parts of the mats through all layers. Machine the binding strips (2″ x 15 1/2) one to the top of the mat and one to the bottom. Trim all extra seam allowance to 1/2″, then turn over binding to the wrong side, giving a good 1/2″ edging, and slip stitch in place on wrong side in the usual way. Repeat with strips 2″ x 13″ on each side.

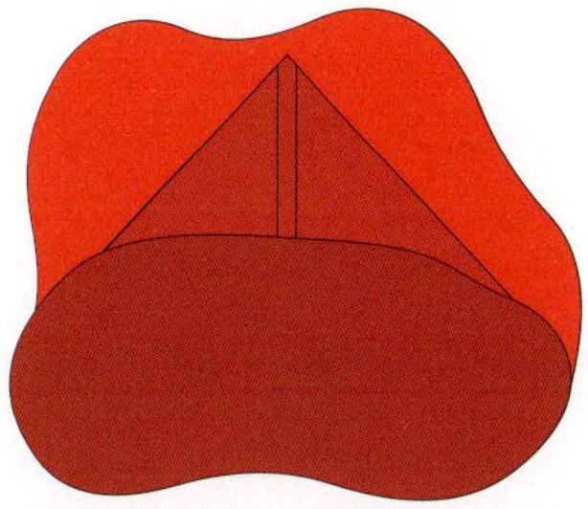

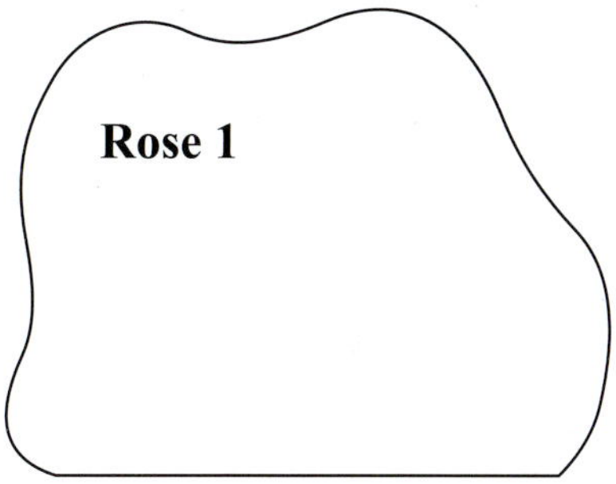

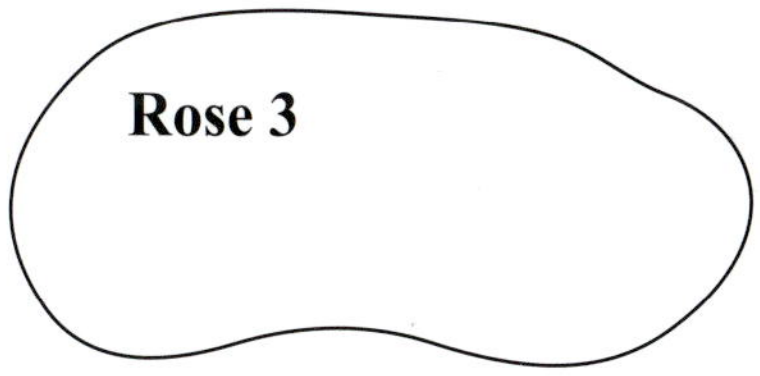

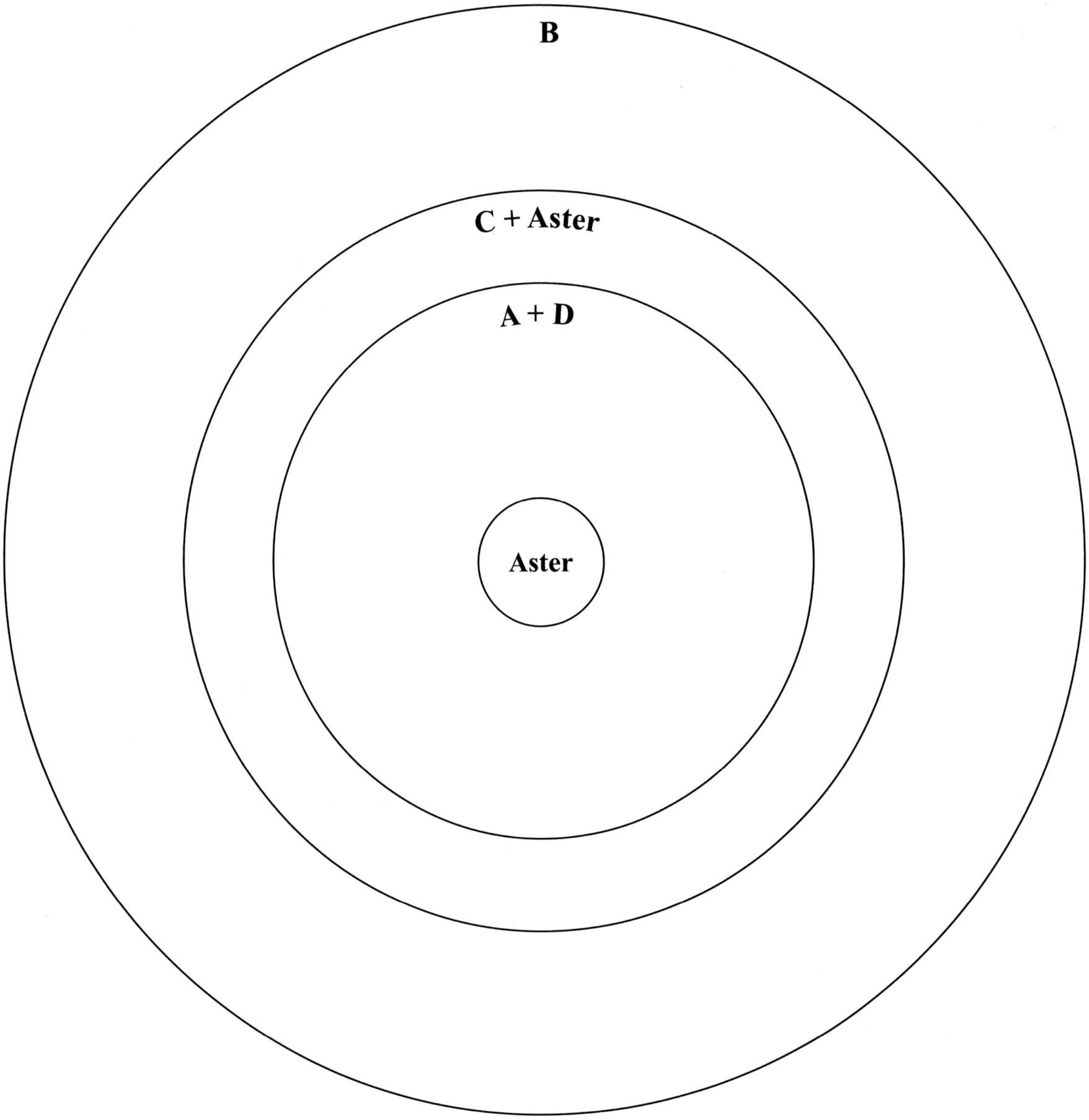
B
C + Aster
A + D
Aster

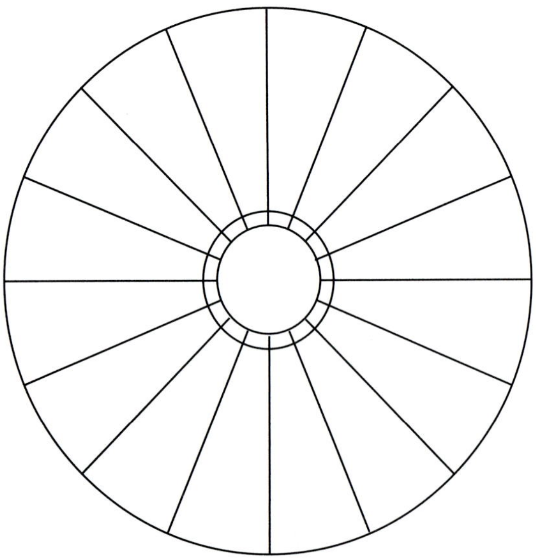

Frühling

Spring

Sommer

Summer

Herbst

Autumn

Winter

Alternative

Diese vier Designs habe ich ursprünglich für meinen Wandbehang *The Circling Seasons* gemacht. Der Wandquilt besteht aus vier Teilen, für jede Jahreszeit eines. Die selben Blumen, nur in größerer Zahl, finden dort Verwendung. Außerdem wurden die applizierten Kreise auf vielfältige Weise mit allerhand Perlen und Goldfäden bestickt und verziert. Das würde sich für Tischsets nicht eignen. Am Kopfende jedes Teils ist eine Sonne in den verschiedenen Farben der Jahreszeiten. Die Sonnenstrahlen sind mit Perlen bestickt. Die Tischsets sind im Grunde genommen eine verkleinerte Variante dieses Quilts.

Alternative

These 4 designs originated from a wallhanging I made called 'The Circling Seasons'. This consists of 4 panels each denoting a season. The same flowers appear in greater number and the remainder of each panel has bias binding circles but treated in many different ways, which would not be suitable for place mats, e.g. bead embellishments. At the top of each panel is a sun illustrating a colour for each season with bead-embellished rays. The place mats are simply a scaled down version of the whole of this wallhanging.

Zufriedene Katzen   Contented Cats Wallhanging

51 x 51 cm (20" x 20")

Zwei Katzen schauen aus einem warmen, gemütlichen Raum durchs Fenster auf eine kalte ungemütliche Landschaft. Die Katzen können von Hand oder mit der Maschine appliziert werden. Dieser kleine Quilt wurde ganz schnell direkt auf das Vlies und die Rückwand maschinenappliziert. Natürlich kann noch zusätzlich gequiltet werden. Das Fensterkreuz kann mit Fertig-Schrägstreifen oder selbst hergestellten Schrägstreifen appliziert werden.

Two cats gaze out through the window from a comfortable and warm room onto a bleak and cold outlook. The cats can be appliquéd by hand or machine and the window frame is constructed using either commercial bias 1/4" tape or why not make your own using the instructions at the beginning of this book. Please note that the wallhanging is machine stitched onto the wadding and backing in a quilt-as-you-go piece. Extra quilting can of course be added if so wished.

Stoffbedarf

Landschaftsmotiv für Hintergrund:
1 Quadrat von 30,5 cm (12")
Dunkle Borte:
4 Streifen von 4 x 112 cm (1 1/2" x 44")
Hellere Borte:
2 Streifen von 6,5 x 112 cm (2 1/2" x 44")
Große Katze: 12 x 19 cm (5" x 7 1/2")
Kleine Katze: 9 x 15 cm (3 1/2" x 6")
Fensterbögen: 1 Quadrat von 17 cm (7")
Rückwand: 1 Quadrat von 56 cm (22")
Vlies: 1 Quadrat von 56 cm (22")
Schwarze aufbügelbare oder selbstgemachte Schrägstreifen (0,6 cm breit)
Vliesofix oder Steam-a-Seam

Schablonen herstellen, rechte Seite markieren.

Schneiden und nähen

Klebevlies auf die linke Stoffseite der Stücke für die Katzen und die Fensterbögen bügeln (Gebrauchsanleitung des jeweiligen Produkts beachten). Die entsprechenden Schablonen seitenverkehrt auf das aufgebügelte Klebevlies legen und Konturen nachzeichnen. Den Fensterbogen einmal mit der rechten und einmal mit der linken Seite aufzeichnen. Auf der Linie ausschneiden. Papier entfernen und auf die oberen Ecken des Landschaftshintergrunds bügeln. Den Hintergrund senkrecht in die Hälfte falten, um die Mitte zu bestimmen. Die Rückwand mit der rechten Seite auf den Tisch legen. Das Vlies genau darauf legen. Den Landschaftshintergrund genau in der Mitte des Vlieses platzieren. Feststecken. Schrägstreifen genau auf die senkrechte, markierte Mitte legen und festnähen. Je nach Belieben mit Zick-Zack-Stich oder einem Blindstich durch alle Lagen. Von oben her etwa 11,5 cm (4 1/2") abmessen und die Querlinie des Fensterkreuzes einzeichnen. Schrägstreifen aufnähen. Dabei sollten die Enden jeweils 0,5 cm (1/4") in die Fensterbögen hineinragen, aber nicht mehr. Von der linken unteren Ecke aus einen Schrägstreifen entlang des Landschaftshintergrunds bogenförmig an den Fensterbögen vorbei bis zur rechten unteren Seite applizieren. Dabei aber einen Abstand von 0,6 cm (1/4") zur Kante lassen als Nahtzugabe für die Borte. Schmale dunkle Borte ansetzen. Dabei sollte die Borte genau an die Schrägstreifen stoßen und

Fabric requirements

Background: 12" (30.5 cm) – square – scenery
Inner and outer borders: dark 4 strips of 4 cm x 112 cm (1 1/2" x 44")
Main patterned border: 2 strips of 6.5 cm x 112 cm (2 1/2" x 44"))
Large cat: 19 cm x 12 cm (5" x 7 1/2")
Small cat: 15 cm x 9 cm (3 1/2" x 6")
Window walls: 17 cm x 17 cm (7")
Backing: 56 cm x 56 cm (22")
Wadding: 56 cm x 56 cm (22")
Black iron on or sew in 1/4" wide bias binding
Bondaweb or Steam-a-Seam 2

Make templates

Method

Iron Bondaweb or Steam–a-Seam 2 to wrong side of the two 'cat' fabric pieces and 'window walls' fabric. Using relevant templates reversed, draw round each shape on the back of the fusible web. For window walls draw one reversed, then turn template over for second side. Cut out on the lines of the two window walls. Remove backing of fusible web and iron in place at two top corners of scenery fabric. Tack wadding onto wrong side of backing fabric. Place the background scenery fabric centrally onto the wadding.

On the scenery fabric measure vertically the half way point between the two sides and make pencil marks all the way up – at approximately 2" intervals. Lay the bias tape on top of these marks and machine stitch both sides of the tape, either with top stitching, zig-zag or hem stitch, whichever method is preferred. Measure horizontally 5" down from the top scenery edge and make pencil marks as before from one window edge across to the other – make sure the tape extends about 1/4" into these window wall edges but not right across. Sew tape as before. Next sew the tape within the first inner border from the bottom left, all round the arched window shape to the bottom right catching the ends of the vertical and horizontal tapes.

Make sure the tape touches the seam edge of the inner border so that no background fabric

kein Hintergrund dazwischen mehr zu sehen sein. Die breitere Borte genauso ansetzen, dann die letzte Borte.

Die Katzen genau auf der Linie ausschneiden, Papier entfernen und links und rechts vom Fensterkreuz auf die erste untere Borte platzieren als würden sie auf einer Fensterbank sitzen. Festbügeln und mit einem engen Zick-Zack-Stich festnähen. Dabei ein farblich passendes Garn benutzen. Einfassen, Tunnel anbringen und fertig ist ein schneller Wandbehang.

shows. Sew 1 1/2" inner border strip along 4 sides catching in the ends of the bias tape.

The middle main border strips can now be added in exactly the same way as the inner border, around all four sides in a clockwise direction. Lastly sew on the outer border strip, all round as before.

Cut out the two cat shapes on the line, position either side of the bias tape central window frame as if they were sitting on a window sill. Remove fusible webbing backing, lightly press in place with an iron.

Using a zig-zag machine stitch – either satin stitch or slightly wider if preferred, and matching thread, appliqué all around edges of cats.
Finally sew narrow binding fabric strips to right side of edges, fold over and slip stitch to back. Attach a suitable sleeve for hanging.

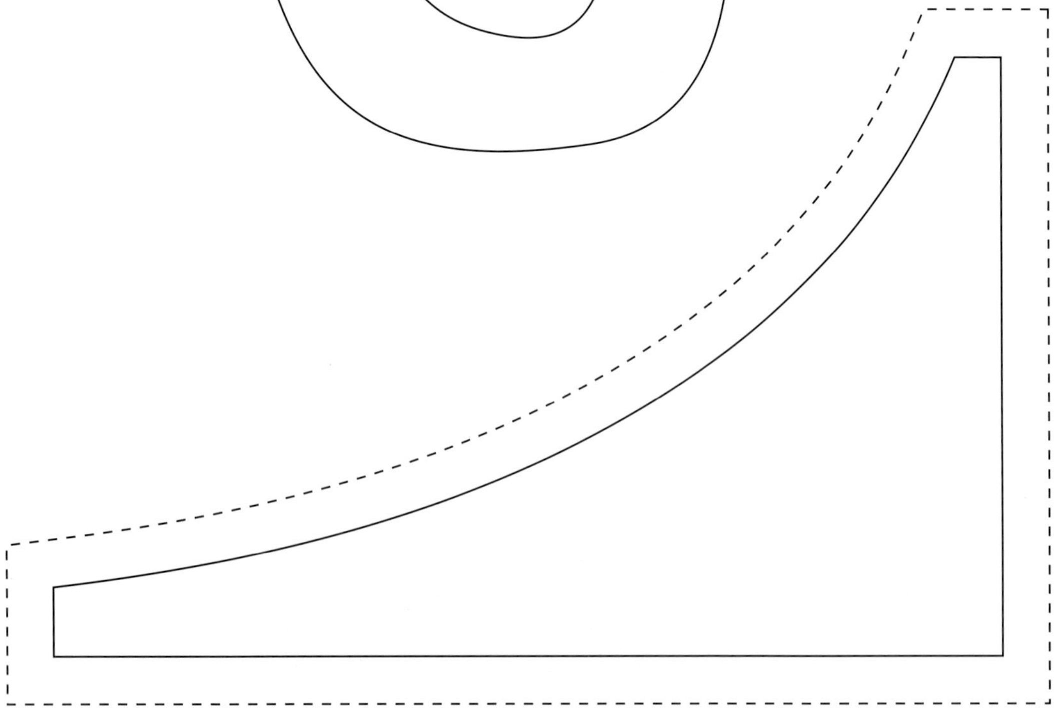

Alternative

Topflappen mit dem größeren Katzenmotiv. Aber beide Schablonen könnten als Applikationsvorlage für die verschiedensten Anwendungen dienen, beispielsweise für ein Brillenetui oder als Block in einem Kinderquilt.

Alternative

Potholder, using larger of cat templates, but both could be used in many other alternative appliqué ways, e. g. spectacles cases, individual small blocks in child's quilt.

Sterne Tischläufer

Ein einfaches Sternenmuster kann durch die Verwendung von Schrägstreifen verändert werden. Die drei Blocks im Tischläufer sind gleich, sehen aber durch die verschiedenen Stoffe aus einer Stoffserie sehr unterschiedlich aus. Natürlich könnten auch alle Blocks vollkommen identisch sein. Gestreifte Stoffe ergeben wunderbare selbst gemachte Schrägstreifen und erzeugen einen interessanten Effekt. Dieser Läufer ist von Hand genäht.

Appliqué Stars Table Runner

A simple star design can be altered with self-made bias. The three blocks in the table runner are identical but look very different when three fabrics from the same line are used. The three blocks could of course be identical if preferred. Striped fabric produces wonderful self-made bias and creates an interesting effect.

35,5 x 132 cm (14" x 52")

Stoffbedarf

Sternenhintergrund: 3 verschiedene einfarbige Quadrate von je 23 cm (9") und 1 Quadrat (für die Läuferenden) von 19 cm (7 3/8"), dieses einmal diagonal teilen.
Sterne: 3 verschiedene gemusterte Stoffe von je 30,5 x 35,5 cm (12" x 44") oder 1 Stoff von 35,5 x 110 cm (14" x 44").
Streifenstoff (Schrägstreifen und Sternzacken): 50 cm (20")
Läuferhintergrund: 30,5 x 110 cm

Schablonen herstellen, zum Handnähen ohne Nahtzugabe, zum Maschinennähen mit Nahtzugabe.

Schneiden

Streifenstoff: mit Schablone A 12 Teile. Schrägstreifen von 2 cm (3/4") Breite (fertiges Maß 0,6 cm (1/4"). Es wird eine Gesamtlänge von mindestens 2,60 m (100") für die Blocks und Dreiecke benötigt und 3,30 m (125") für die Einfassung. Die einzelnen Schrägstreifenlängen innerhalb der Blocks sind mit 18 cm (7") ausreichend lang, für die Enddreiecke genügen Längen von 23 cm (9"). Für die Einfassung muss angesetzt werden.
Gemusterter Stoff: 2 Stücke mit Schablone D für die Läuferenden.

Pro Block

Gemusterter Stoff: 1 Teil mit Schablone B, 4 Teile mit Schablone C, 2 Streifen von 3,8 x 26,7 cm (1 1/2 x 10 1/2"), 2 Streifen von 3,8 x 23 cm (1 1/2" x 9")
Sternenhintergrund: 4 Teile mit Schablone E.

Läuferhintergrund

Die benötigten Trennstreifen haben eine Breite von 6,5 cm (2 1/2"). Insgesamt wird eine Länge von ca. 4 m (160") gebraucht. Man kann einen Streifen in dieser Länge vorbereiten und jeweils die benötigte Länge abschneiden.

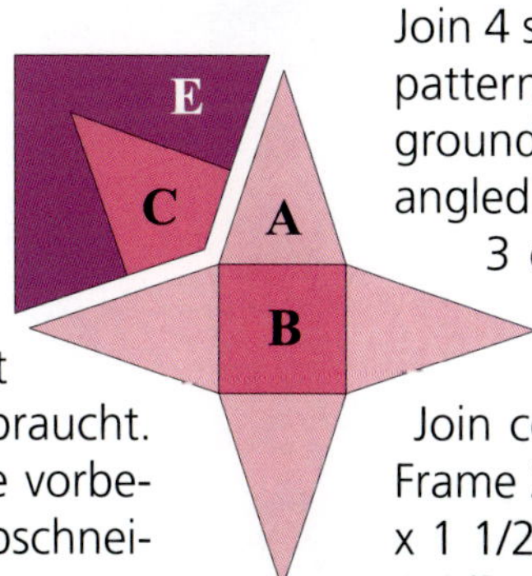

Fabric requirements

3 patterned fabrics: 12" x 14" (same fabric may be used 3 times if preferred in which case a piece 14" x 44" is required)
3 plain background fabrics: 9" x 9", plus a single piece 8" square.
Striped fabric for bias strips: 20"
Sashing fabric: 44" x 12"

Make templates.

Cutting

Striped fabric: 12 pieces from template A. Cut bias strips 3/4" wide. A length of at least 100" will be needed for blocks and triangles and 125" for binding. Block lengths need to be 7" long, end triangles' lengths 9" and binding lengths can be joined.

Each Block

Patterned fabric: 1 template B, 4 template C, 2 straight strips 10 1/2" x 1 1/2", 2 straight strips 9" x 1 1/2".
For end triangle cut 2 from template D.

Plain or background fabrics: 4 pieces from template E, 1 square 7 3/8", cut diagonally across to provide 2 triangular end shapes.
Plain Sashing: a total of 176" x 2 1/2" straight strips, which may be joined at any point to provide necessary lengths.

Method – Each Block

Join 4 striped A pieces to centre square B. Centre patterned C pieces diagonally on top of background E pieces approximately 1" from right-angled corner. Tack in place. Repeat with other 3 corners of blocks. Cover raw edges of C pieces with prepared bias strip, folding at top, and appliqué in place.
Join corner units to A/B unit to make 9" x 9". Frame 2 opposite sides with patterned strips –9" x 1 1/2", then remaining 2 sides with 10 1/2" x 1 1/2" strip.
Repeat for remaining 2 blocks.
End Triangle Shapes – place patterned fabric D onto background fabric triangles, centrally and

Nähen pro Block

4 gestreifte Dreiecke A an das Mittelquadrat B nähen. Die gemusterten Dreiecke C so auf das Hintergrundstück E platzieren, dass die Spitze ungefähr 2,5 cm (1") von der rechtwinkligen Ecke entfernt liegt. Feststecken. Die offenen Kanten mit Schrägstreifen bedecken und festnähen. Genauso mit allen Ecken verfahren. Die fertiggestellten Ecken an den Stern nähen. Die kurzen gemusterten Streifen jeweils links und rechts an diesen Block nähen, dann die langen Streifen oben und unten. Mit den anderen Blocks genauso verfahren.

tack in place. Cover raw edges of patterned fabric with bias stripe strips and appliqué in place.

Join 3 blocks and two end triangles together with plain sashing, straight strips 10" x 2 1/2".

Join 2 plain sashing strips to each end of runner, mitering points. Complete sashing each side with a 44" x 2 1/2" strip (join where necessary to make required length).

Prepare Backing and wadding to match top. Bind with remaining bias strip, joining as necessary, and mitering at both ends and corners.

Enddreiecke

Je ein gemustertes Dreieck D auf ein Enddreieck platzieren, feststecken. Die offenen Kanten mit Schrägstreifen bedecken und zusammen applizieren.

Blocks und Enddreiecke mit Trennstreifen verbinden. Die Enddreiecke mit Trennstreifen einfassen, dabei die Spitzen der Enddreiecke mit Briefecken schließen. Die Streifen an den Enden auf das Läufermaß zurückschneiden. Lange Streifen an den langen Kanten ansetzen, die Enden abschrägen. Wie gewohnt einreihen, quilten und einfassen.

Quilten

Es wurden die Konturen aller Sterne und applizierten Dreiecke nachgequiltet. Die Trennstreifen wurden mit Hilfe der Quadrateschablone F mit einem Raster versehen.

Quilting

In-ditch quilting round all shapes of each block, including either side of the patterned fabric frames. Likewise end triangles.

Using quilting template F on point, mark and quilt whole area of sashing.

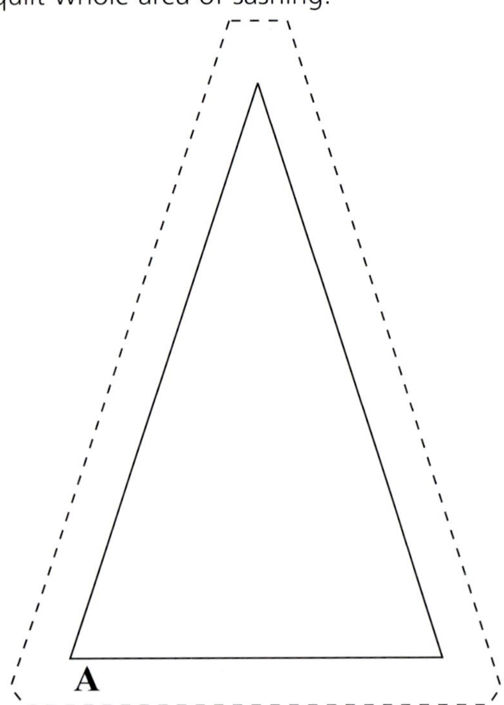

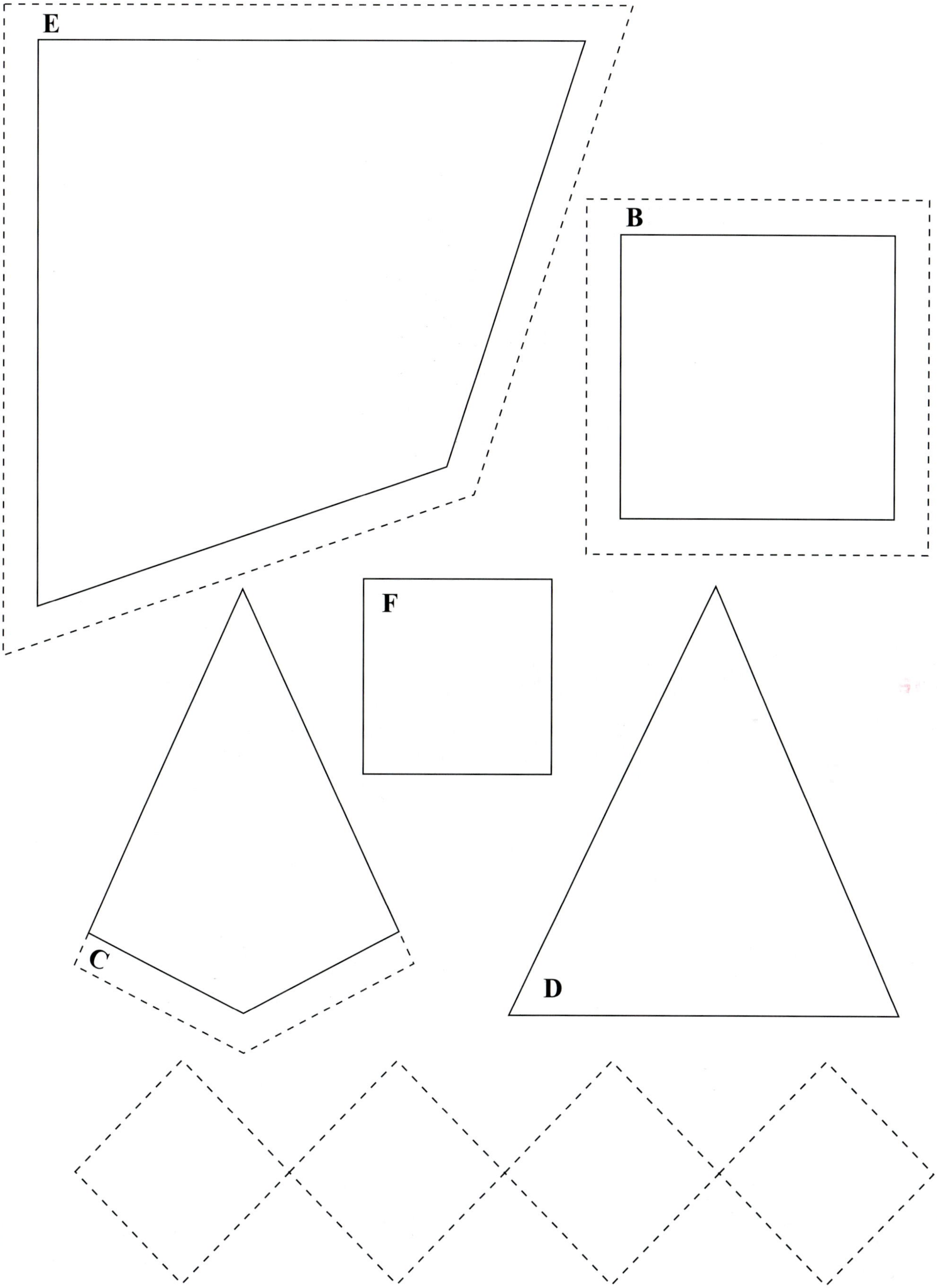
E
B
F
C
D

Herbststerne

Autumn Stars Quilt

134,6 x 190,5 cm (53" x 75")

Eigentlich sollte dieser Quilt nur die Alternative zum Tischläufer darstellen, da er aber der Titelquilt ist, bieten wir hier auch die vollständige Anleitung an.
In diesem Quilt wechseln sich zwei Blocks miteinander ab, ein großer und ein kleiner Stern, wobei die Blocks jeweils auf die Spitze gestellt

Since this quilt is the cover quilt we will not simply mention it as alternative but give you full instructions for it. There are two blocks involved alternately with each other and placed on point. In the original quilt every block is made with different fabrics and the colours are graded from yellow through orange and rust to dark brown.

sind. Im Originalquilt sind alle Blocks aus unterschiedlichen Stoffen gearbeitet und die Farben wechseln von Gelb über Orange zu Rost und Dunkelbraun. „Frühlingssterne" könnten von Gelb über Grün bis Blau changieren. „Sommersterne" wären schön in einem Verlauf von hellem Gelb über Orange, Rot bis hin zu Lila. Eine weitere Alternative wäre es die großen Sterne alle gleich zu machen und die kleinen Sterne anders als die großen, aber auch gleich. Dies sind nur einige zusätzliche Anregungen und es gibt noch viele Möglichkeiten.

Der **Stoffbedarf** wird nur für jeweils einen Block angegeben, da mit Resten gearbeitet wurde.

1 großer Stern

Blockgröße: 20,3 x 20,3 cm (8" x 8"), insgesamt werden 24 benötigt:
Hintergrund: 28 x 28 cm (11" x 11")
Sternenstoff 1: 28 x 65 cm (11" x 56")
Sternenstoff 2: 28 x 28 cm (11" x 11")

1 kleiner Stern

Blockgröße: 20,3 x 20,3 cm (8" x 8"), insgesamt werden 15 benötigt:
Hintergrund: 25,5 x 25,5 cm (10" x 10")
Sternenstoff 3: 8 x 25,5 cm (3" x 10")
Blockeinfassung: 10 x 25,5 cm (4" x 10"), hieraus 4 Streifen von 2,5 x 25,5 cm (1" x 10") schneiden

Eck- und Seitendreiecke

1 Quadrat von 25,5 cm (10")
1 Quadrat von 18 cm (7")
3 Streifen von 2,5 x 25,5 cm (1" x 10")

Borte: 90 cm (1 yard)

Schneiden und nähen

Großer Stern

Sternenstoff 1: 4 Teile mit Schablone A, 1 Quadrat mit Schablone B und 4 Teile mit Schablone F ausschneiden, dabei Nahtzugabe zugeben.
Sternenstoff 2: 4 Teile mit Schablone E, 4 Teile

"Spring" Stars could involve grading from yellow through green to blue. "Summer" Stars could be graded in brighter yellows through oranges, reds to purples. Alternatively all large star blocks could be the same and likewise the small star blocks. These are just a few additional suggestions and the choices are many.

Fabric requirements

are given for just one large star block and one small star block as only scraps are involved.

1 Large Star Block

8" x 8" (24 required in total):
Background: 11" x 11"
Star fabric 1: 11" x 22"
Star fabric 2: 11" x 11"

1 Small Star Block

8" x 8" (15 required in total):
Background: 10" x 10"
Star fabric 3: 3" x 10"
Contrasting fabric for block edging: 4" x 10", cut in 4 strips of 1" on the straight

Corner and Side Settings

10" x 10" will make 2 side setting triangles
7" x 7" will make 2 corner setting triangles
2 strips 1" x 10" for each side triangle
1 strip 1" x 10" for each corner triangle

Border: 1 yard

Method

Large Star Block

Using star fabric 1 cut 4 pieces with template A and 1 piece with template B, please add seam allowances. Using star fabric 2 cut 4 pieces with template E and 4 with template F, add seam allowances. Appliqué the 4 'E' pieces around all sides of square B, matching straight raw edges. Sew 4 'A' pieces to centre square.

mit Schablone F ausschneiden, Nahtzugabe nicht vergessen. 4 Teile mit Schablone C, dabei nur an den kurzen Seiten Nahtzugabe zugeben. Die langen Seiten genau auf der Linie ausschneiden.
Die 4 Teile E entlang der Kanten von Quadrat B applizieren. Die vier Teile F aus Sternenstoff 2 auf 4 Dreiecke A applizieren und diese an das Mittelquadrat nähen.
Hintergrund: 4 Teile mit Schablone D ausschneiden. Teile C wie in der Abbildung auf die Hintergrundstücke D platzieren. Einreihen. Mit den Schrägstreifen die langen Kanten bedecken und fest nähen. Den Schrägstreifen an den Spitzen scharf knicken und falten. Die Hintergrundstücke von Hand an den Mittelstern nähen. Die Teile F aus Sternenstoff 1 auf die Teile C applizieren.

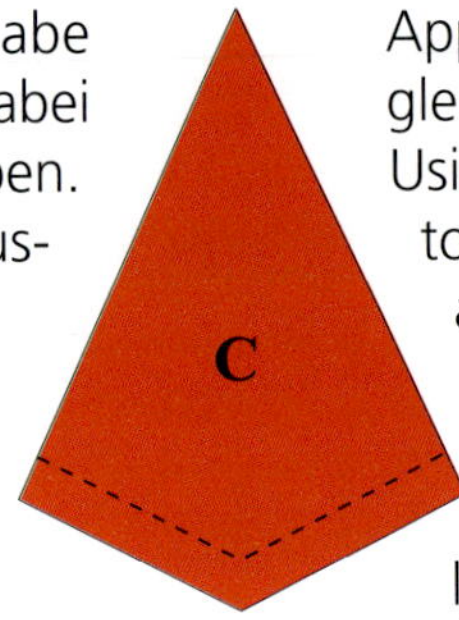

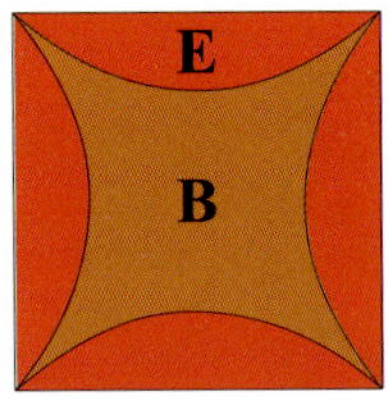

Appliqué lozenges F centrally to each 'A' triangle.
Using fabric 2 cut out 4 with template C, noting to cut exactly on the long upright lines, but adding a 1/4" seam allowance to lower smaller lines.
Using background fabric cut 4 pieces with template D. Tack template C pieces centrally on to background D pieces.
With 4 bias strips cut from fabric 1 appliqué to raw edges of C piece, folding over sharply at top of C.
Using 1/4" seams join background corners to square/triangle piecing, sewing along one edge to the centre first then turning fabric to sew along second side.
Lastly, using fabric 1, cut 4 lozenges with template F and appliqué to background corner/triangles.

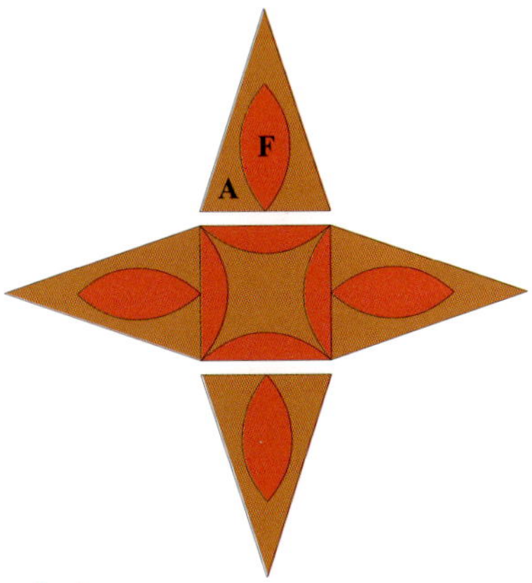

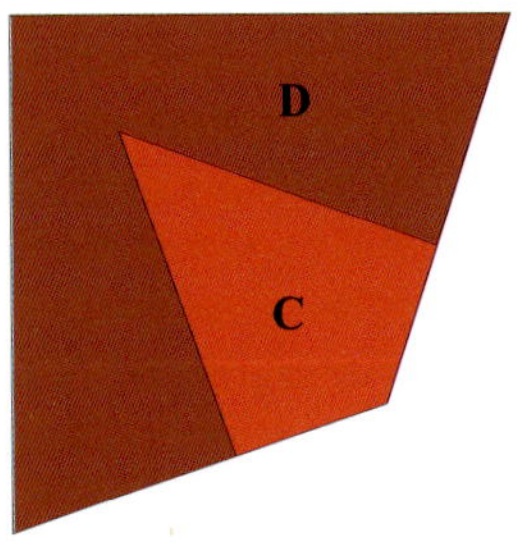

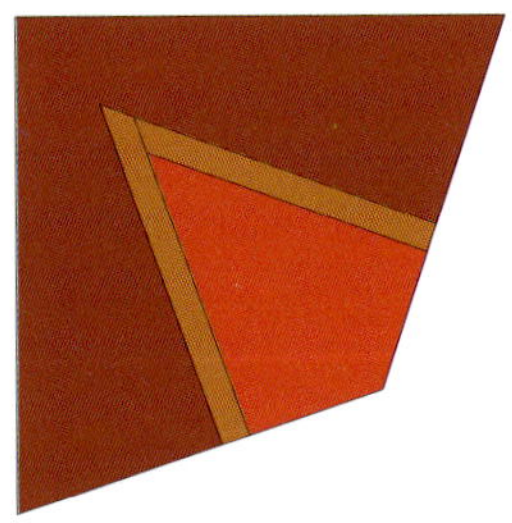

Kleiner Stern

Hintergrund:
1 Quadrat von 21,6 cm (8 1/2")
Sternenstoff 3: 4 Teile mit Schablone G ausschneiden, Nahtzugaben zugeben, an den kurzen Kanten zu einem Stern verbinden. Mittig auf den Hintergrund platzieren und applizieren. Die vier Streifen für die Blockfassung links auf links jeweils der Länge nach in die Hälfte falten und mit den offenen Kanten auf die Blockkanten legen. Die gefaltete Seite auf den Hintergrund applizieren.

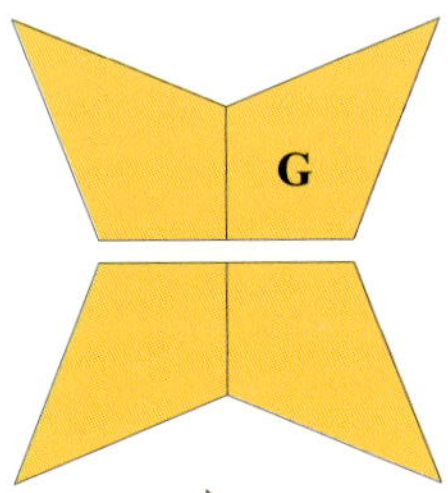

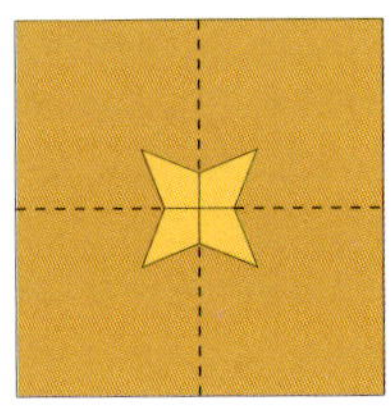

Small Star Block

Trim background fabric to 8 1/2" x 8 1/2" square. With fabric 3 cut 4 pieces with template G. Join lower edges in pairs, then a four to make a star.

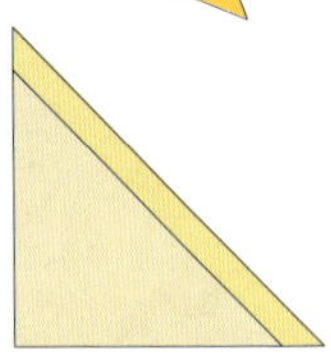

Turn under remaining longer edges and appliqué centrally to background square. Take the 4 block edging strips, fold in half lengthwise and tack all round 4 sides, matching raw edges together. Appliqué folded edges to background fabric.

Eck- und Seitendreiecke

Die Quadrate jeweils einmal diagonal teilen, so dass Dreiecke entstehen. Die Streifen der Länge nach links auf links falten und auf die Kanten der Dreiecke applizieren, die im Quilt innen liegen werden.

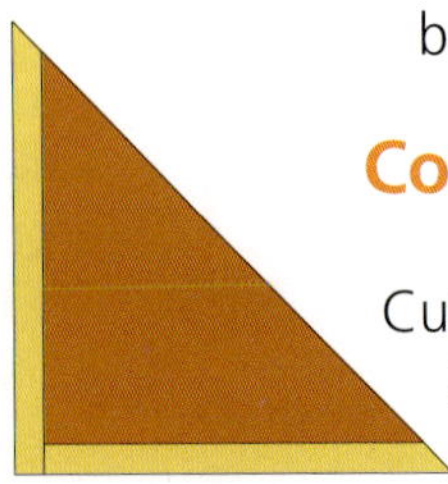

Corner and Side Settings

Cut the 10" squares in half diagonally to make 2 triangles from each. Take the 1" edging strips, fold in half lengthwise as for Small

Die Blocks zusammen mit den Dreiecken in diagonalen Reihen anordnen und reihenweise zusammennähen.

Star Block above and add to 2 sides only, appliquéing folded side to side triangles. The remaining long side of each triangle with the raw edges will be joined into the border.
The 4 corner setting triangles are made the same way from the 7" squares, but this time only the one long side has the folded strip added.

Assembly

The blocks should be put together in diagonal rows with the blocks on point.
Lastly cut border fabric into 4 1/2" wide strips (joining where necessary) and join firstly to sides, then to top and bottom of central quilt piece.

Borte

Die Streifen für die Borte sind 11,5 cm (4 1/2") breit. Den Quilt in der Höhe und Breite jeweils genau ausmessen und die Streifen auf die entsprechende Länge zuschneiden. Zuerst die seitlichen Streifen ansetzen, dann oben und unten.

Hier einige Quiltvorschläge

Für ein gutes Bortenmuster verwenden Sie Schablone C und zwei Quiltlinien und Schablone F in der Mitte.

Suggested Quilting Designs

For a good border design use template C with 2 lines of quilting, and template F in the centre.

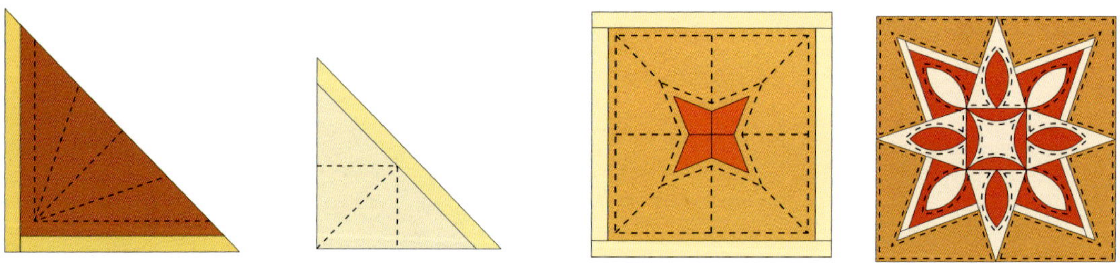

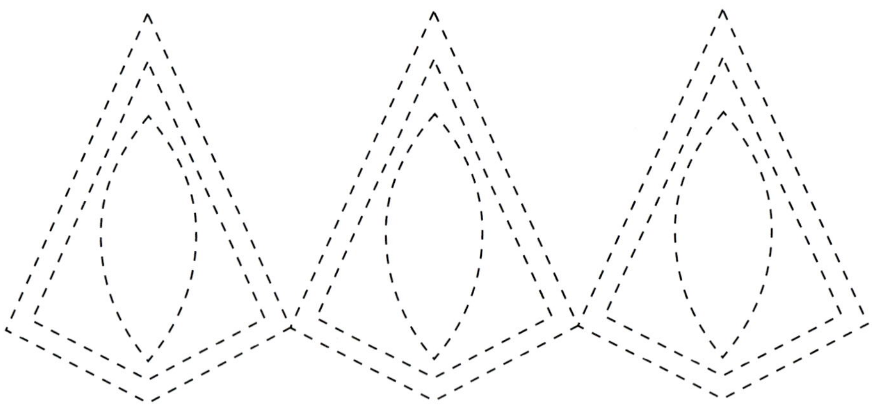

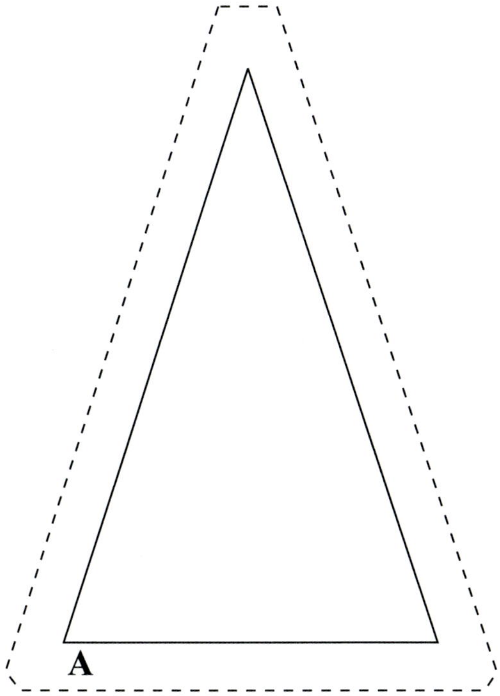
A

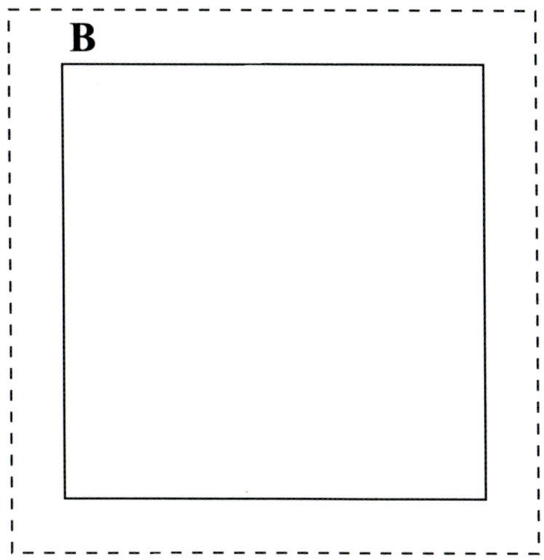
B

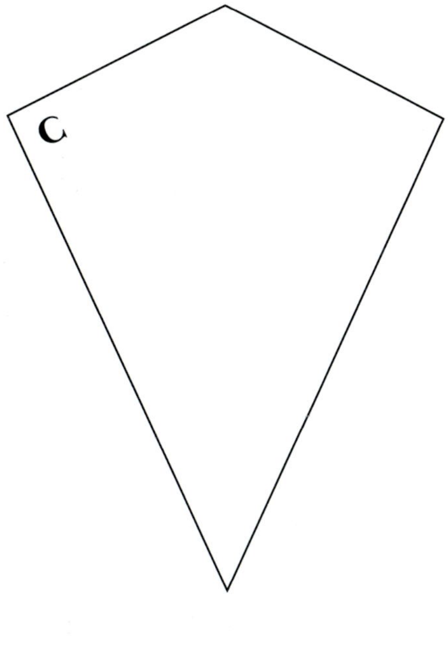
C

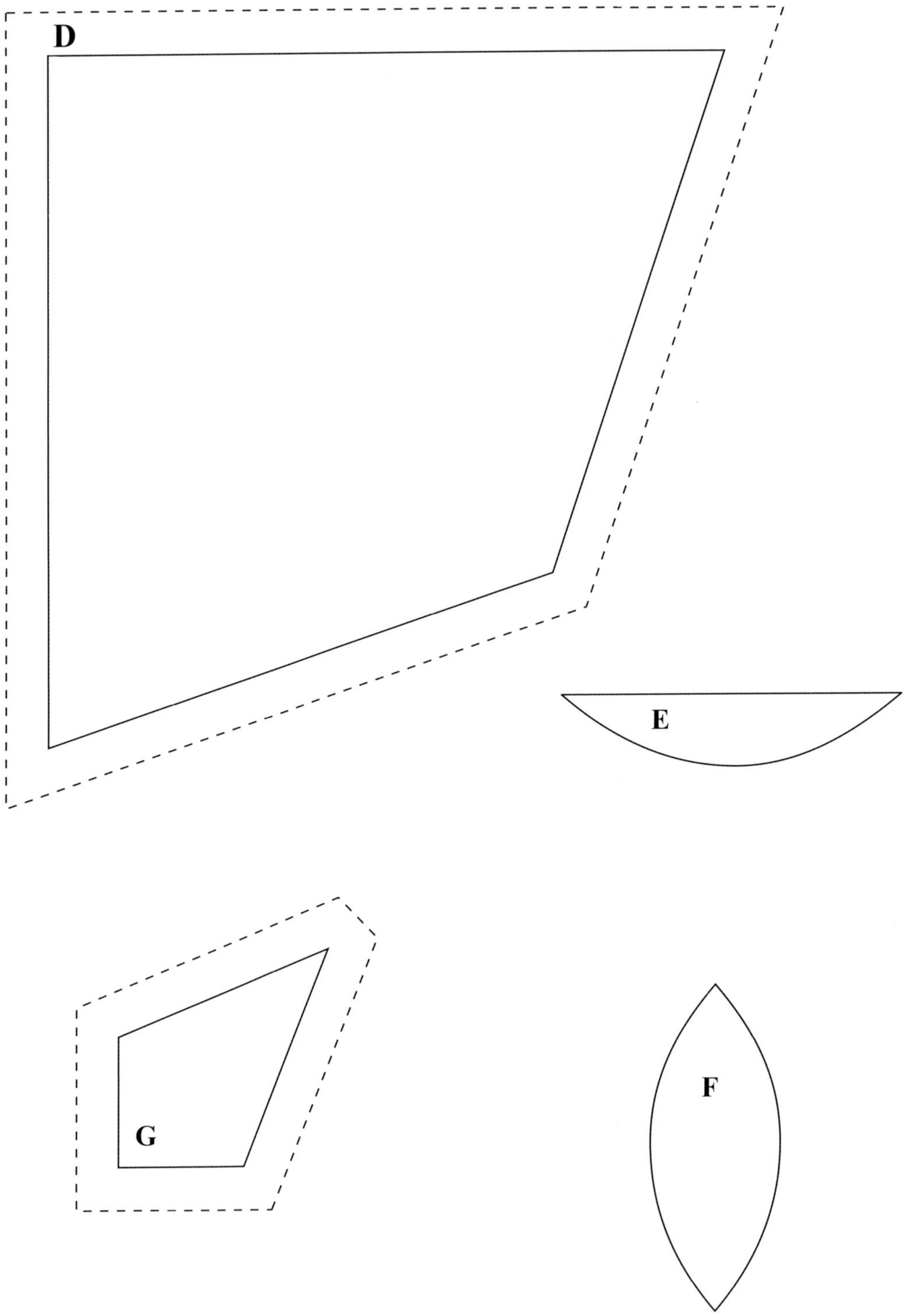
D
E
G
F

53,5 x 117 cm (21" x 46")

Kurvige Streifen

Gestreifte Stoffe wurden für die applizierten, lang gezogenen Ovale in diesem Wandbehang verwendet. Die Formen wurden in Kreisen und Bögen angeordnet, so dass die Streifen aussehen wie Wellenlinien. Die Hintergrundquadrate und -rechtecke bestehen aus verschiedenen, kontrastierenden Farben. Für die Ovale wurden acht verschiedene Streifenstoffe benutzt. Während der Hintergrund unbedingt ein Schachbrettmuster haben sollte, könnten die Ovale auch alle aus nur einem Streifenstoff bestehen.

Curved Stripes

Striped fabrics are used in an appliqué lozenge shape in this wallhanging and arranged in circles and curved lines, giving the impression that stripes can bend. The background squares and rectangles are in different but contrasting colours and eight different striped prints. The background also needs to have a 'chequered' look but just 1 striped print could be used throughout even for the circles and for the swags.

Stoffbedarf

Hintergrundquadrate: 16 Quadrate von 14 cm (5 1/2″), wobei immer zwei gleiche helle und zwei gleiche dunkle zu einem Viererblock genäht werden.
Rechtecke:
16 Stück von 14 x 7,5 cm (5 1/2″ x 3″), immer ein helles und ein dunkles bilden ein Paar.
Ovale: 8 verschiedene Streifenstoffe, jeweils ca. 10 x 50 cm (4″ x 20″)
Borte: 30 x 110 cm (12″ x 44″)

Schablone herstellen.

Schneiden

Streifenstoffe: Für die seitlichen Bögen aus vier verschiedenen Stoffen jeweils 12 Ovale ausschneiden. Nahtzugaben nicht vergessen. Für die Kreise aus vier verschiedenen Stoffen jeweils 8 Ovale ausschneiden. Dabei die Schablone mit den Spitzen in Richtung der Streifen auflegen.
Borte: 4 Streifen von 7,5 cm (3″) Breite

Nähen

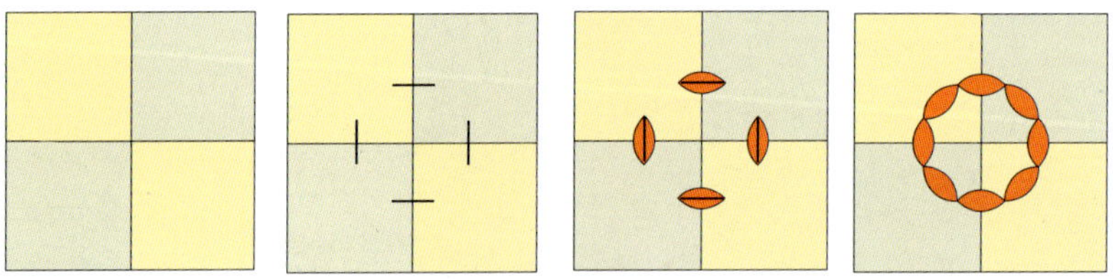

Immer aus 4 Quadraten einen Viererblock nähen. Vom Mittelpunkt aus gemessen im Abstand von 5 cm (2″) eine Markierung auf jeder Nahtlinie anbringen. Darauf jeweils ein Oval für einen Kreis platzieren und festnähen. Die übrigen Ovale für den Kreis in die Lücken platzieren und applizieren. So mit allen Viererblocks verfahren. Die Blocks zusammennähen. Immer 8 Rechtecke im Wechsel hell-dunkel zu einem Streifen zusammensetzen und seitlich an die Quadrateblocks ansetzen. Dabei darauf achten, dass jeweils ein helles Rechteck an ein dunkles Quadrat stößt und umgekehrt. Die Ovale bogenförmig immer im Wechsel auf den Rechtecken und den Quadraten anordnen und applizieren.

Fabric requirements

Background squares: 4 sets of dark/light squares 11″ x 11″ in 2 co-ordinated colours for each
Side rectangles:
4 sets of dark/light pieces 11″ x 5 1/2″ in 2 coordinated colours for each
Lozenges: 8 different striped fabrics – 1 for each circle and 1 for swags on both sides.
Border: 12″ x 44″

Make templates.

Cutting

For each set of 4 cut squares 5 1/2″ x 5 1/2″
For each set of 4 cut rectangles 5 1/2″ x 3″
Take the lozenge template and for 4-square + 4-rectangle block cut 8 appliqué shapes for each circle, placing template vertically to match direction of stripe and 6 appliqué shapes for each side rectangle, again placing template vertically to match direction of stripes.

Method

Join each set of 4 squares in a chequer-board arrangement.
On each set of 4 make a mark 2″ from centre on each seam.
Take 4 of the circle lozenges, centralize them on each mark and appliqué in place
The remaining circle lozenges should fill the gaps.
Repeat for all 4 square blocks. Join sets together and add the rectangles by sewing each side separately in alternating colours
Repeat for second side then join each rectangle strip to main body of squares.
Make marks as before 2″ from centre but this time alternating the mark in the rectangle then in the square, forming a swag. Appliqué a centre lozenge then fill in the gaps as before, but taking the lozenge to a joined corner.

Zwei gegenüberliegende Bortenstreifen ansetzen, dann die anderen beiden. Die Streifen sind mit Briefecken angesetzt, so dass die Streifen etwas länger als die eigentliche Quiltlänge zugeschnitten werden müssen.
Wie üblich einreihen und quilten.

Quilten

Zum Quilten wurde die größere Ovalschablone benutzt. Damit wurde an den Kreuzungspunkten der Quadrate außerhalb der Kreise eine Art Kleeblatt markiert und innerhalb der Kreise ebenfalls ein Kreis. Auch die Konturen der Kreise und Bögen wurden beidseitig nachgequiltet.

Continue the swag along both sides of central squares.

Border

Cut border fabric 3″ wide, joining where necessary, and attach to each side first, then top and bottom.

Quilting

The lozenge quilting template is slightly larger than the appliqué one and can be used for quilting patterns. In the pictured wall hanging the area between the squares is quilted centrally and in the centre of the circles. Also quilt around the circles and swag shapes.
See if you can use the lozenge quilting template in other arrangements.

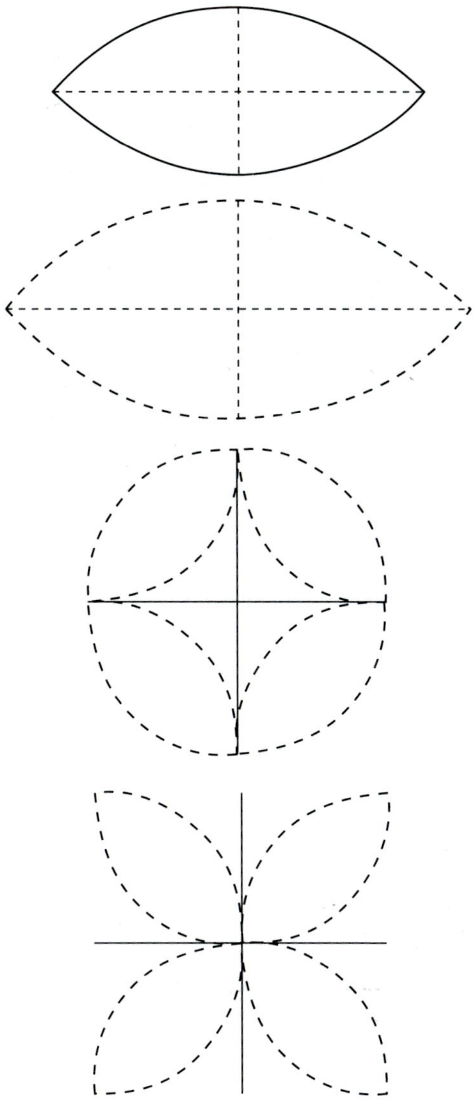

Alternative

In dem hier gezeigten größeren Wandbehang wurden ebenfalls gestreifte Ovale appliziert. Außer den Kreisen und Bögen wurde für die Borte noch eine Girlande mit den Ovalen erzeugt. Es ist sehr interessant wie viele verschiedene Muster man mit dieser einfachen Form gestalten kann.

Alternative

The larger wallhanging pictured here features exactly the same method of appliqué lozenges using striped fabric. You will notice, in addition to the circles and swags used in the small wallhanging, ovals, wavy lines and a different swag. It is interesting to discover all the different effects this method can produce.

Tanzende Blätter

Dancing Leaves Quilt

124,5 x 124,5 cm (49" x 49")

Dieses Blättermotiv kann als Windmühle im Block oder linienförmig in der Borte verwendet werden, sowohl als Applikations- als auch als Quiltmotiv. Die applizierten Blocks haben alle einen cremefarbenen Hintergrund, während die gequilteten Blocks aus vielen verschiedenen Farben bestehen. Sicher könnte man sich in den Farben auch beschränken und dadurch einen ganz anderen Effekt kreieren. Die Applikationen können von Hand oder mit der Maschine ausgeführt werden.

This leaf shape can be used either in blocks or in a straight line as in the border, as an appliqué motif or as a quilting template. The block backgrounds are all cream prints and the quilted squares are marbled fabrics. I have used different colours throughout but of course a more restricted colour palette would produce a different effect. The appliqué can either be by hand or machine.

Stoffbedarf

Blockhintergrund: 13 verschiedene cremefarbene Quadrate von 20,3 cm (8"), insgesamt 61 x 110 cm (24" x 44")
Einfarbige Quadrate: 12 verschiedenfarbige von 20,3 cm (8"), insgesamt 61 x 110 cm (24" x 44")
Blätter: Reste (mindestens 15 x 25 cm/ 5" x 10")
Eckquadrate: 4 Quadrate von 15,2 cm (6")
Breite Borte: 1 m (40")
Schmale Borte und Einfassung:
61 x 110 cm (24" x 44")

Schablone herstellen.

Schneiden und nähen

Pro Block: 4 Blätter mit Hilfe der Schablone markieren und ausschneiden. Zum Handapplizieren die Nahtzugabe nicht vergessen. Blätter vom Quadratemittelpunkt aus arrangieren und applizieren.

Immer im Wechsel einen applizierten Block und ein farbiges Quadrat zu einer Reihe von 5 Blocks zusammenfügen. Die zweite Reihe mit einem farbigen Quadrat beginnen. Die schmale Borte hat eine Breite von 3,8 cm (1 1/2"). Je einen Streifen links und rechts, dann oben und unten anfügen. Die breite Borte hat eine Breite von 15,2 cm (6"). Es ist hilfreich zuerst die Blätter zu applizieren, bevor die breite Borte angesetzt wird. Dazu das Quiltoberteil inklusive schmaler Borte der Länge nach genau ausmessen und die breite Borte auf dieses Maß zuschneiden. Pro Seite werden 10 Blätter benötigt. Die Mitte der Borte sowohl der Länge nach als auch in der Breite markieren. Die Linie wird durch die Blätter überdeckt. Von der Mitte ausgehend fünf Blätter in die eine Richtung platzieren und festnähen und fünf Blätter in die andere Richtung. Auf die Eckquadrate 4 Blätter windmühlenförmig anordnen, dabei zeigen die Spitzen in die Ecken, und festnähen. Zwei Bortenstreifen mit den Eckquadraten verlängern. Zuerst die kurzen Streifen links und rechts ansetzen, dann die langen Streifen oben und unten. Wie üblich einreihen und quilten.

Fabric requirements

Block background: 13 different 8" squares in cream prints or 24" x 44" in same fabric
Marbled prints: 12 different 8" squares or 24" x 44" for quilted squares in same fabric
Appliqué leaves: a selection of scraps (minimum 5" x 10")
Border: 40"
Corner squares: 4 x 6"
First border and binding: 24" x 44"

Make template

Method

Cut sets of leaves for each cream print background square – 4 to each square. With hand appliqué remember to add a seam allowance for turning. Arrange leaves on each square centrally and appliqué in place.
Using the same template and the same leaf arrangement, lightly mark the quilting design on each marbled 8" square.
Assemble blocks, alternately the appliqué squares and the squares for quilting. Join one row at a time then sew rows together to form main body of quilt.
Cut first border fabric across width in 4" x 1 1/2" strips and join to main body of quilt, two sides first, then top and bottom.
The main borders can be appliquéd before adding to the quilt, which makes the sewing easier. Each border needs 10 appliqué leaves and the border fabric should be cut – 38" x 6". Measure the middle point of the borders lengthwise and draw a line lightly (this will be covered by the appliqué later). Starting at the centre of each border appliqué 5 leaves one direction and 5 the other way, placing appliqué pieces on the drawn line. Repeat for each border.
Take the 4 corner blocks and appliqué 4 leaf motifs as before, but this time in a diagonal formation.
Join corner blocks to each end of 2 of the borders.
Join 1 border to each of the sides of the main quilt. Then join the borders with the corner squares attached to the top and bottom. Cut the remaining binding fabric into 3" strips. Joining where necessary, for the edging of the quilt after the quilting.

Quilten

Die farbigen Quadrate mit dem Blättermotiv bequilten. Die applizierten Blätter umquilten, ebenso die Konturen der Blätter auf der Borte.

Alternative

Dieses Blatt ist ein sehr vielseitiges Applikationsmotiv. Es kann in vielen Bereichen Verwendung finden. So zum Beispiel auf einer Tasche. Es wurde vergrößert, um als Mittelquadrat auf beiden Seiten einer Tasche dienen zu können.

Quilting

The leaf motif marble squares can now be quilted on the marked pattern lines. The appliqué blocks may be quilted around the shapes, likewise the border leaves. On the border, quilt 1/4" in from the inner sashing and the binding.

Alternative

This is a good motif to use for appliqué at any time. The tote bag uses the same, but enlarged shape for a central panel on both sides of the bag. The motif itself can be enlarged or reduced as necessary to fit a design.

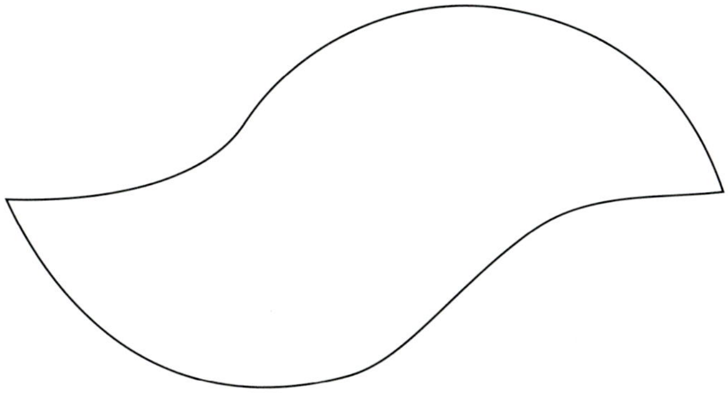

Keltisches Kissen

Celtic Cushion

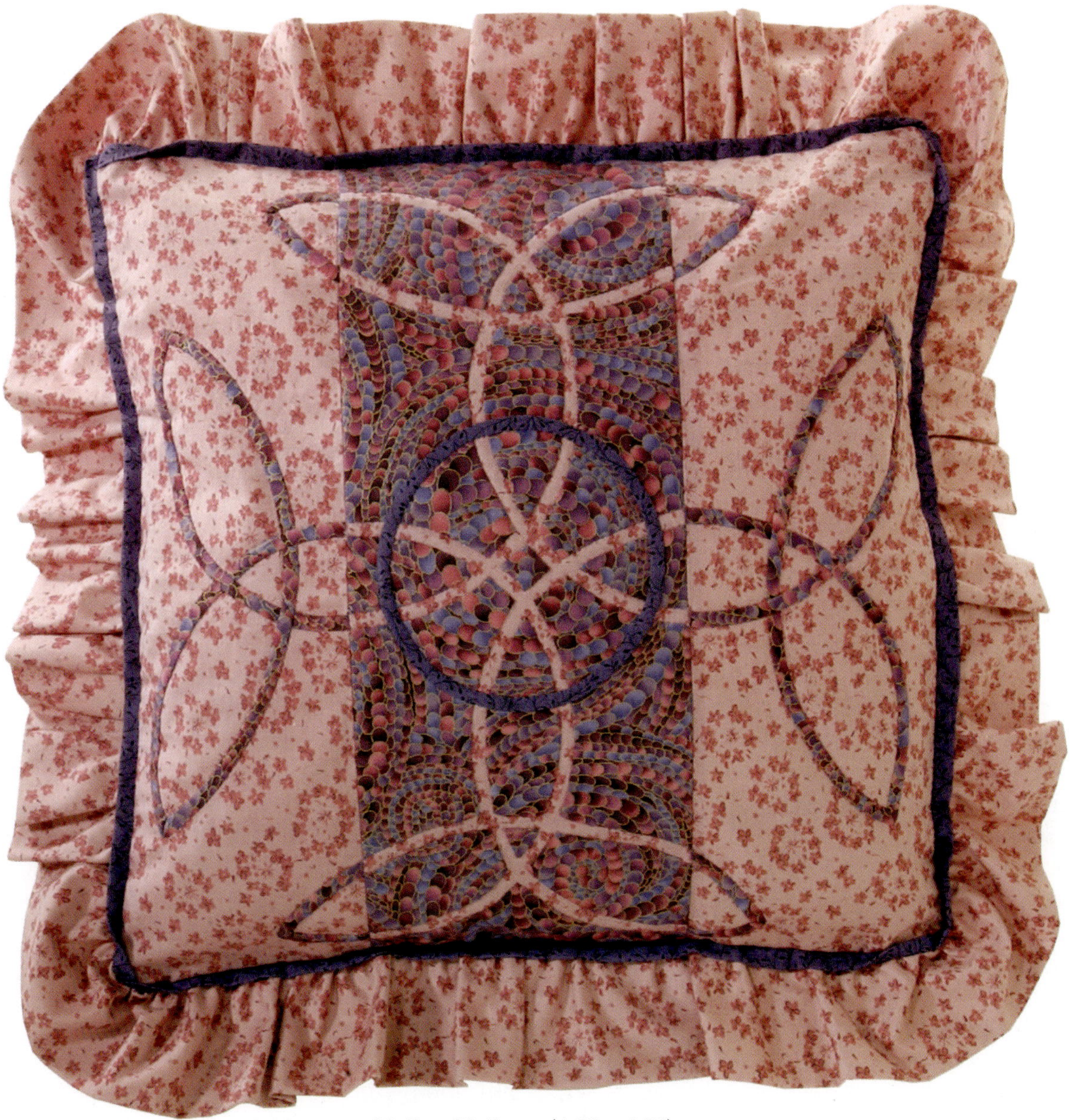

40,5 x 40,5 cm (16" x 16")

Dieses Design basiert auf dem klassischen keltischen Muster „Lover's knot" (Knoten der Liebenden). Es wurde mit selbstgemachten Schrägstreifen und einem plötzlichen Farb- und Technikwechsel ausgeführt. Statt mit Schrägstreifen wird das Muster jäh mit der Reversapplikation fortgeführt. Ich habe das Kissen mit einer Biese und Rüsche fertiggestellt, aber das muss nicht sein. Es könnte genauso gut ohne jeden Zierrat geschlossen werden.

This design is based on the basic 'lovers knot' Celtic pattern with appliqué self made bias but on the fabric change across the middle the method changes to reverse appliqué while still following the original pattern lines. I have added a frill and inserted a folded fabric trim, but this is optional and could be left with a straight plain edge.

Stoffbedarf

Hauptfarbe (hier Pink): 46 x 50 cm (18" x 19 1/2"), 3 Streifen von 12,7 x 110 cm (5" x 44")
Kontrastfarbe 1 (hier Lila): 16,5 x 46 cm (6 1/2" x 18"), 1 Quilters Viertel für Schrägstreifen
Kontrastfarbe 2 (Mittelkreis, Biese, Rückseite): 50 x 110 cm (20")
Fixier-Stickvlies: 40,5 x 40,5 cm (16" x 16")

Schneiden und nähen

Hauptfarbe: 3 Rechtecke von 16,5 x 46 cm (6 1/2" x 18"), eines davon mit dem passenden Kontrastrechteck links auf rechts legen, d. h. die Schauseiten liegen bei beiden Stücken oben. Das Kontrastrechteck liegt obenauf. Einreihen. Mit den beiden anderen Rechtecken so zusammennähen, dass das eingeriehene Stück in der Mitte liegt. Nahtzugaben in Richtung Mittelstück bügeln.
Kontrastfarbe 2: 2 Streifen von 2,5 x 110 cm (1" x 44") der Länge nach links auf links falten und bügeln für die Biese.
Das keltische Motiv auf Fixier-Stickvlies übertragen. Stickvlies auf die rechte Seite des Kissenmittelstücks legen und fixieren. Mit der Nähmaschine auf den Musterlinien nähen. Stickvlies entfernen. Schrägstreifen herstellen (0,6 cm (1/4") fertige Breite) und auf die Musterlinien der Seitenstücke applizieren, dabei die Fäden der Musternaht nach und nach entfernen. Die Enden der Schrägstreifen in der Naht zwischen Mittelstück und Seitenstück verstecken. Dazu die Nähte ein kurzes Stück öffnen, Enden der Schrägstreifen dazwischen schieben und Nähte wieder schließen.
Im Mittelstück die Musternähte nach und nach aufschneiden und die Kanten mit unsichtbaren Applikationsstichen versäubern. Es kommt der Hauptstoff zum Vorschein. Vom zweiten Kontraststoff einen Schrägstreifen von 50 cm (20") Länge herstellen und als Mittelkreis auf das Mittelstück applizieren. Die Enden zusammennähen. Die Kissenplatte auf 43 x 43 cm (17" x 17") zurückschneiden.

Rüsche und Biese

Für eine Rüsche den Umfang der Kissenplatte ausmessen und diese Zahl mit 1,5 multiplizieren. Einen Streifen in dieser Länge herstellen. Dazu

Fabric requirements

Main fabric: 18" x 19 1/2", 3 strips 5" x 44"
Contrast Fabric: 18" x 6 1/2"
Bias strips: fat quarter
2nd contrast fabric for folded insert in seam and circular appliqué: 2 strips 1" x 44", folded lengthwise. 20" for bias strips 20" long for circle and cushion back.
Stitch and Tear (or similar lightweight paper)
14" Zipper

Method

Cut main fabric into 3 pieces 18" x 6 1/2". Tack together one main fabric and the contrast piece – contrast on top and background piece face upwards underneath. Treat this as a single piece. Join 3 strips across the 18" width – background main fabric, tacked contrast, background main fabric. Press seams towards centre tacked piece. Trace Celtic pattern onto Stitch and Tear, centre onto machined piece above, pin and tack if necessary. Then machine stitch along lines. Tear away paper and Celtic pattern is left.
Make bias strips. Appliqué centrally onto pattern lines on top and bottom pieces of cushion panel, removing pattern lines as you go, about 1" at a time. Extend bias strips 1/4 " at central contrast piece, undo stitching at point of meeting for 1/4", tuck ends of bias into seam and re-stitch.
For central panel cut on stitched pattern line for about 2" at a time, again removing pattern stitches as you progress. Slip stitch each side of cut line, exposing background main fabric. Make bias from second contrast fabric approximately 20" long. Appliqué centre circle bias strip, joining where 2 ends meet.
Trim cushion to 17" square. Make a frill 1 1/2 times the outside measurement of the cushion by joining the 3" x 5" wide lengths all together, fold in half lengthwise. Using a long length stitch on the machine at the raw edges, gather up the frill to fit on to the cushion edges. Sew to the cushion edges inserting also into the seams the 1" 2nd contrast folded strip.
The back of the cushion can be made from the remaining 2nd contrast fabric, either with a zipper or any other preferred method of fastening, then the front is stitched to the back, right sides together, and taking care not to catch the frill in the stitching.

die 3 Streifen aus der Hauptfarbe zusammennähen und der Länge nach links auf links falten. Die Stichlänge der Nähmaschine sehr groß einstellen und entlang der offenen Kanten nähen. Die Rüsche auf die benötigte Länge zusammenziehen. Beim Annähen auch die Biese mit einarbeiten. Die Rückseite des Kissens aus der restlichen Kontrastfarbe 2 herstellen, entweder mit Reißverschluss oder einem Hotelverschluss.

Dazu die Teile für die Rückseite rechts auf rechts auf das Vorderteil legen. Beim Zusammennähen auf die Rüsche achten.

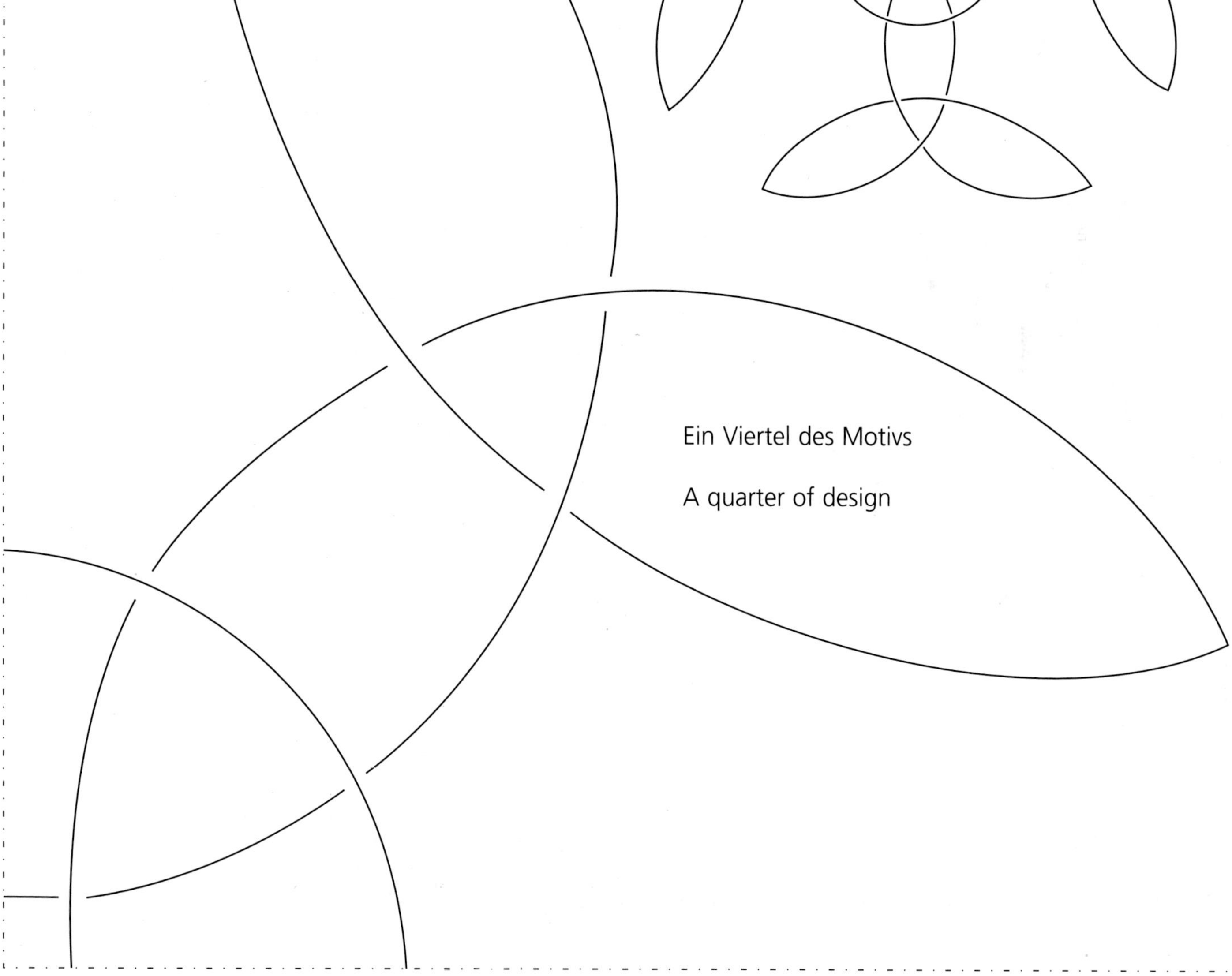

Ein Viertel des Motivs

A quarter of design

Alternative

Dieser interessante Technikmix kann in beliebig vielen Blocks verwendet werden. Für einen großen Bettenquilt könnte man beispielsweise keltische Musterblocks mit einfarbigen Stoffquadraten abwechseln, in denen ein keltisches Muster gequiltet wird.

Alternative

This double appliqué idea can be used in any number of blocks in any Celtic design and incorporated into a bed quilt with the addition of quilted Celtic patterns or plain areas.

Verrückter Ohio Stern   Crazy Ohio Star Wallhanging

81,5 x 81,5 cm (32" x 32")

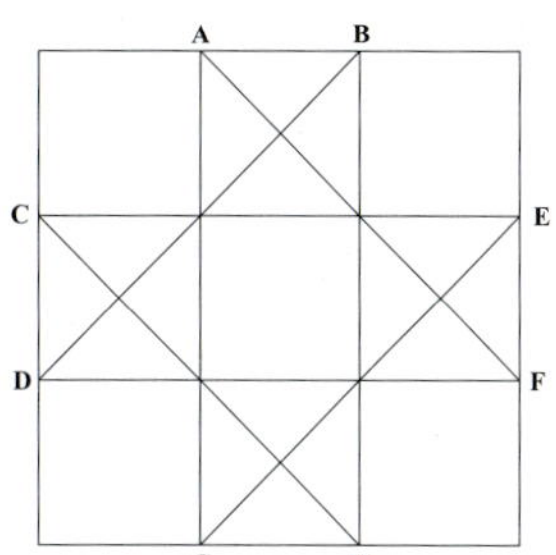

Dies ist die ideale Gelegenheit, die Restekiste ein bisschen zu entlasten. Jeder Sternenblock in diesem Block besteht aus vier verschiedenen Stoffen. Ein traditioneller Ohio Stern Block ist hier abgebildet, aber wenn man die von A-H markierten Spitzen willkürlich verschiebt, entsteht ein verzogener Stern. Auf Seite 77 sehen Sie, mit welcher Vorlage ich gearbeitet habe. Sie dient Ihnen gleichzeitig als Schablone. Nur die Nahtzugabe müssen Sie bei jedem einzelnen Teil noch zugeben. Alle Teile sind unterschiedlich. Natürlich könnte man diesen Wandbehang auch mit dem traditionellen

This is a great opportunity to use up some of the fabric stored away in scrap bags! Each pieced block in this wallhanging uses 4 different fabrics. A standard Ohio Star patchwork block is pictured here, but if the marked points A to H are moved randomly a distorted version of the block emerges. A picture on page 77 shows the effect I worked on and the component parts of the block can be used as templates – there are no two the same! Of course the wallhanging could be made from the Standard Ohio Star block, but perhaps not so much fun. Add on appliqué squares to the plain blocks and borders to make a bright and very unusual wallhanging.

Ohio Stern Block nähen, aber das wäre sicher nicht so lustig. Die Quadrate auf den schwarzen Hintergrundblocks und der Borte sind appliziert.

Stoffbedarf

Viele Reste in Schablonengröße, meist nicht größer als 15 cm (6"). Für die Sternenhintergründe einen einfarbigen oder leicht gewölkten Stoff nehmen, aber für die Sterne möglichst viele verschiedene bunte Stoffe benutzen. Insgesamt werden 12 Sternenblocks gebraucht.
Dunkler Stoff für Quilthintergrund und Borte: 70 cm (27 1/2")
Quadrate: 4 verschiedene Farben, je 25 x 25 cm (10" x 10")
Dünne Pappe oder sehr festes Papier, daraus 28 Quadrate von 3,8 cm (1 1/2") schneiden

Schablonen herstellen, dabei Nahtzugabe zugeben, und unbedingt, wie vorgeschlagen, nummerieren.

Schneiden und nähen

Alle Teile mit der Nummer 1 sind für den Hintergrund. Alle Teile mit der Nummer 2 sind aus einem Stoff, alle Teile mit Nummer 3 sind aus einem anderen Stoff und Teil 4 besteht wieder aus einem anderen Stoff. Beim Auflegen der Schablonen auf die linke Stoffseite unbedingt darauf achten, die Schablonen jeweils auf die Rückseite zu drehen, damit die Stoffstücke später nicht spiegelverkehrt sind und zueinander passen. Sicherheitshalber die Schablonen wie ein Puzzle auslegen und immer nur zum Markieren des jeweiligen Stoffes wegnehmen. Gleich wieder an seinen Platz zurücklegen. Genauso mit den ausgeschnittenen Stoffstücken verfahren, damit es nicht zu Verwechslungen kommt.
Die Stücke wie bei einem normalen Stern auch erst in kleineren Einheiten zusammennähen, dann reihenweise, die Reihen schließlich zum Block.

Tipp

Da alle Stücke im schrägen Fadenlauf geschnitten werden, ist es hilfreich, alle Stoffe mit Stärke zu behandeln, um ein Verziehen der Stücke einzudämmen.

Fabric requirements

Many scraps of fabric, probably no bigger than 6" square. Use plain or marbled for the star surround but be as bright and varied as possible for the other parts of the block. There are 12 pieced blocks in total.
Dark fabric for appliqué block backgrounds, border and binding: 27 1/2" (70 cm)
Appliqué squares in 4 different colours: 10" x 10" pieces
Stiff paper or thin card

Make templates.

Method

As mentioned in the first paragraph, make templates for all the parts of the distorted block. Number them as shown. All the templates with the number 1 are from the same fabric (preferably plain or marbled). All templates numbered 2 are from a second fabric, templates numbered 3 from a third fabric. Whilst template 4, the centre, is yet another fabric. It is most important to number all templates clearly and to remember to REVERSE them on the wrong side of the fabrics when marking them. It is a good idea to lay out the templates in 'jigsaw fashion' and to pick them up when marking the fabric and replacing them in their place before picking up the next. Likewise when cutting out the fabric, place down in the position to be used. This does help considerably in avoiding mix-ups. Cut out all pieces with 1/4" seam allowances. Piecing should be done in rows, exactly as with a normal Ohio Star block. Join the 3 rows and make 12 blocks in total. From the dark fabric cut 4 squares 6 1/2" x 6 1/2". The appliqué has been dealt with in a similar way to English hexagons that is to say over papers. Cut 28 1 1/2" x 1 1/2" squares from thick paper or thin card. Cut 28 fabric squares 2" x 2" in four different fabrics – 7 in each fabric. Place paper squares in fabric squares, turn over seam allowance and tack to papers. Press all fabric squares, remove tacking and gently remove all papers. Draw a diagonal line across the 6 1/2" x 6 1/2" dark fabric squares on RIGHT side and arrange 4 coloured squares on top, starting and ending 1/4" in from sides.

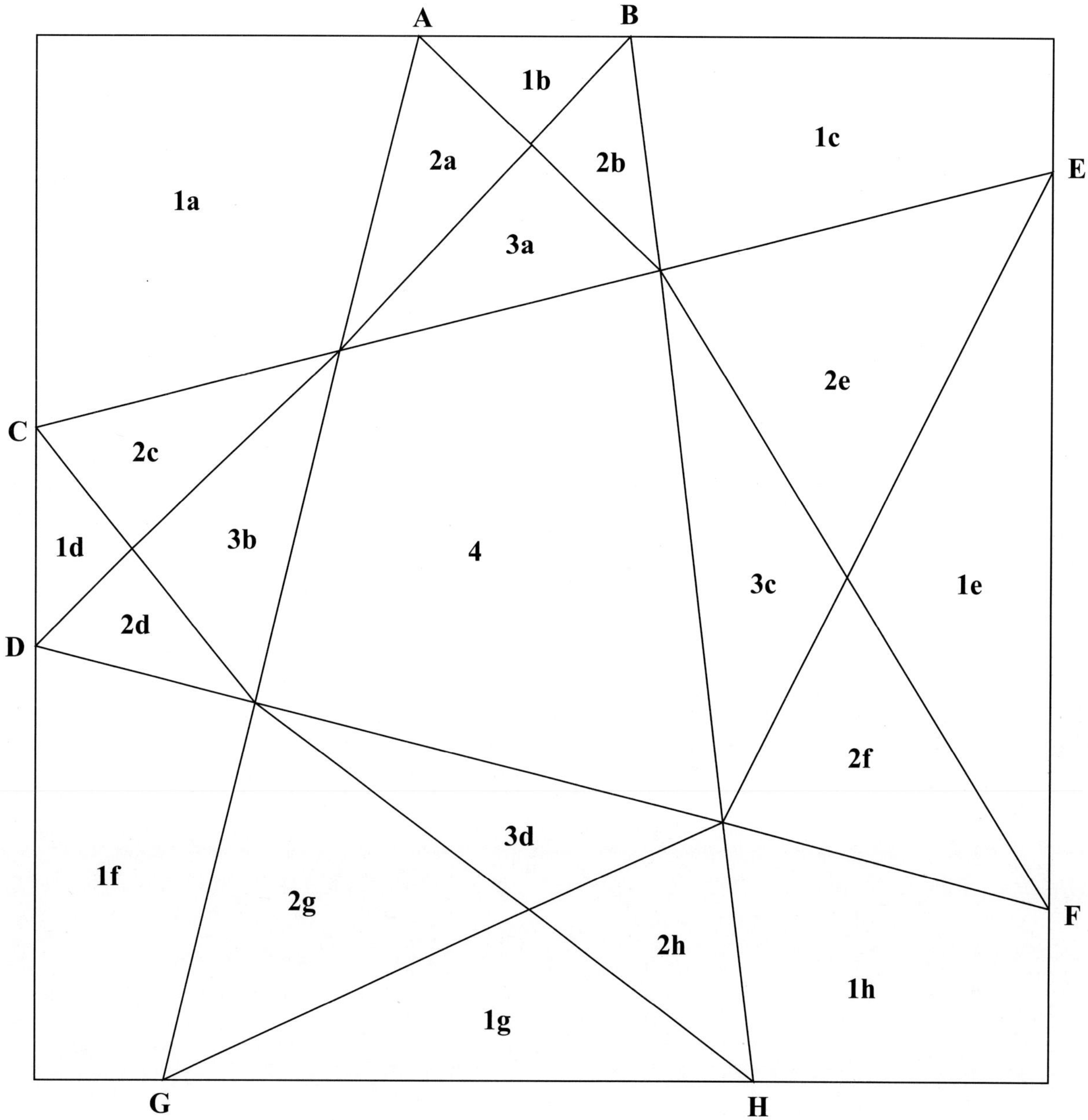
A
B
1b
2a
2b
1c
E
1a
3a
2e
C
2c
1d
3b
4
3c
1e
2d
D
2f
3d
1f
2g
F
2h
1h
1g
G
H

Im BERGTOR VERLAG sind auch folgende Patchworkbücher erschienen:

Herbstquilts von **Claudia Hasenbach.** Von Äpfeln über Blätter bis hin zu allerlei Pilzen, Kürbissen, Bäumen und sogar einer Physalis sind alle nur denkbaren Herbstszenarien in 13 liebevoll ausgearbeiteten Quilts präsentiert. Alle Motive sind auf Papier genäht, einige noch zusätzlich mit kleineren Applikationen ergänzt. Die Technik *Nähen auf Papier* wird ausführlich erläutert. *96 S., 13 komplette Anleitungen, alle Vorlagen in Originalgröße, viele farbige Bilder und Grafiken.*
ISBN 3-937703-08-X, Preis: € 22,–

Schätze aus der Restekiste von **Eli Thomae.** Ihre Restekiste quillt über, aber Sie können sich von keinem einzigen Fitzelchen Stoff trennen? Dann ist dieses Buch genau richtig für Sie. Zu allen 34 verschiedenen Patchworkmustern gibt es eine komplette Anleitung und eine Formel für abweichende Restegrößen, so dass Sie alle Ihre Reste wirklich aufbrauchen können. Das Schönste dabei ist, dass die meisten Quilts ohne Schablonen auskommen, denn Eli liebt es Tricks zu finden, die das lästige Schablonenherstellen unnötig machen.
Voraussichtlich 96 S., 34 komplette Anleitungen, viele farbige Bilder und Grafiken. **ISBN 3-937703-07-1, Preis: € 22,–**

Patchwork Tiere II von **Ula Lenz**
Diesmal gibt es einheimische Tiere wie Igel, Reh und Eule, auch Hunde und Vögel, Enten, Kraniche und Fische. Bunte Papageien und Kakadus, Wildschweine und Hasen. Zwölf Quilts mit Anleitung. Alle Blocks aus allen drei Büchern sind untereinander kombinierbar.
96 Seiten, 21 x 27,5 cm, mehrfarbiger, flexibler Einband, durchgehend farbig, viele Bilder und Grafiken, Vorlagen in Originalgröße. **ISBN 3-937703-06-3, Preis: € 22,–**

Patchwork Tiere von **Ula Lenz**
70 Motive zum Nähen auf Papier. Von urzeitlichen Dinosauriern über Meerestiere bis hin zu heimeligen Bauernhoftieren finden Sie in diesem Buch alles, was kreucht und fleucht. Sei es der heimische Singvogel oder die Libelle auf der Blumenwiese.
96 Seiten, 21 x 27,5 cm, mehrfarbiger, flexibler Einband, durchgehend farbig, viele Bilder und Grafiken, Vorlagen in Originalgröße. **ISBN 3-937703-02-0, Preis: € 22,–**

Blühende Quilts von **Ula Lenz**
Immergrüne Gärten auf Papier genäht. Schöne, einzigartige Blumen- und Tiermotive aus der heimischen Flora und Fauna. Zwölf Quilts mit vollständiger Anleitung zum Nacharbeiten regen zu immer neuen Variationen an. Die Technik Nähen auf Papier wird anschaulich Schritt für Schritt erklärt. *96 Seiten, 21 x 27,5 cm, mehrfarbiger, flexibler Einband, durchgehend farbig, Vorlagen in Originalgröße.* **ISBN 3-9806815-8-0, € 22,–**

Patchwork Party – Zwei Bücher in einem! Über 70 Rezepte und 15 Patchworkprojekte mit ausführlicher Anleitung. Schablonen in Originalgröße. Die Patchworkprojekte in diesem Buch sind schnell genäht und haben größtenteils einen Bezug zu Essen und Küche im weitesten Sinne. *80 Seiten, durchgehend farbig, zahlreiche Fotos und Abbildungen. Praktische, hochwertige Ringbindung.* € 1,– pro verkauftem Buch ist für einen guten Zweck bestimmt.
ISBN 3-937703-00-4, Preis: € 23,–.

Ginies Patchwork Fibel II von **Ginie Curtze.** Die Fortsetzung der ersten Fibel mit 85 neuen Schablonen, Ideen und Geschichten. Ginies Fibel ist kein Anleitungsbuch im üblichen Sinne, sondern ein Ideen- und Anregungsbuch, das den Leser zu eigener Kreativität ermuntern will. Ein Buch, gleichermaßen geeignet für Anfänger und Fortgeschrittene.*80 Seiten, 21 x 27,5 cm, mehrfarbiger, flexibler Einband, durchgehend farbig, mit zahlreichen Bildern und Grafiken.*
ISBN 3-9806815-9-9, Preis: € 23,50

Quilts von **Dorle Stern-Straeter** mit einem Vorwort von **Michael James**
Dorle Stern-Straeter, die renommierteste Quiltkünstlerin Deutschlands, beschreibt ihren Werdegang, ihre Quilts, ihre Arbeitsweise. Bildband und Autobiographie in einem. Deutsch, Englisch, Französisch. *112 Seiten, 21,3x27,5 cm, mehrfarbiger, flexibler Einband, über 70 Quilts, teilweise mit Detailansicht, durchgehend farbig.*
ISBN 3-9806815-0-5, € 15,24

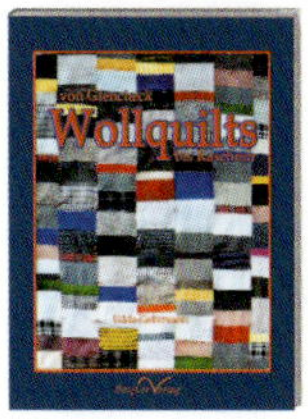

Wollquilts von **Edda Gehrmann** mit einem Vorwort von **Kaffe Fassett**
Bilder von über 70 Quilts machen auch Ihnen Lust, selbst einen außergewöhnlichen, warmen und kuscheligen Quilt zu nähen. Genaue Anleitungen zu sechs wunderschönen Quilts machen es leicht, einen Einstieg zu finden.
144 Seiten, 21 x 27,5 cm, mehrfarbiger, flexibler Einband, durchgehend farbig, mit über 70 Bildern und Grafiken, zweisprachig deutsch-englisch.
ISBN 3-9806815-4-8, € 22,–

Korak von **Ruth Tschudy.** Eine fast vergessene Patchworktechnik, die ganz von Hand gearbeitet wird. Ruth Tschudy beschreibt nicht nur ganz genau wie man einen Korak herstellt, sondern auch, wo er herkommt und verbreitet war. Mit kleinen Übungsstücken werden Sie an den Entwurf eigener Arbeiten herangeführt. *80 Seiten, 21 x 27,5 cm, mehrfarbiger, flexibler Einband, durchgehend farbig, über 60 Fotos, viele Grafiken, genaue Schritt-für-Schritt Anleitungen, zweisprachig deutsch-englisch,*
ISBN 3-9806815-7-2, € 22,-, sFr 43,

Streifentechniken von **Irene Kahmann**
27 Schritt-für-Schritt Workshops und leicht verständliche Anleitungen regen Ihre Kreativität an. Ob geometrische Seminole-Muster, Streifenmuster, Crazy-Patchwork, Kurven oder frei Geschnittenes, lernen Sie wie kompliziert wirkende Muster schnell und einfach zu nähen sind. Einführende Informationen über Material und Basistechniken, den Umgang mit Farben, Strukturen und vieles mehr. Alle Schablonen in Originalgröße. Anregende Quiltgalerie mit Quilts von bekannten deutschen und amerikanischen Quiltkünstlern. *Leicht veränderte Neuauflage, 96 Seiten, Softcover, 21 x 27,5 cm, durchgehend farbig, 200 Bilder.*
ISBN 3-937703-04-7, Preis: € 22,–

Vom Kreis zum Quadrat von **Ranghild Graßhoff** führt in ihrem Arbeitsbuch in die japanische Falttechnik ein und zeigt anhand unzähliger Beispiele die Vielfalt dieser Faltmethode. Ob von Hand genäht oder mit der Maschine, die Variationen lassen sich endlos fortsetzen. Allein mit dem Block *vom Kreis zum Quadrat* lassen sich wundervolle Blüten, Ornamente, Bögen und vieles mehr zaubern. Eine Technik, die süchtig macht und sich wunderbar zum Arbeiten unterwegs eignet. *96 Seiten, Softcover, 21 x 27,5 cm, Schablonen in Originalgröße, Schritt-für-Schritt Anleitungen, ca. 400 Grafiken, durchgehend farbig.*
ISBN 3-937703-05-5, Preis: € 22,–

BERGTOR VERLAG · Beim Bergtor 14 · 67269 Grünstadt
Telefon 0 63 59/20 58 28 · Fax 0 63 59/37 88
www.bergtor-verlag.de